# THE SURVIVOR STORY OF ARNELLE

## A GIRL FROM AFRICA

ARNELLE M. CRUZ

To: Alyssa

The Survivor Story of Arnelle



Wishing you all your dreams come true.

tellwell

Tellwell Talent
www.tellwell.ca

ISBN
978-0-2288-1236-4 (Hardcover)
978-0-2288-1235-7 (Paperback)
978-0-2288-1237-1 (eBook)

# INTRODUCTION

I am from the land called Africa, from a little country called Liberia. It is amazing what I have learned from my past by what I have seen and by what I have been told by others. I am going to make you take the journey with me into my past to make you to understand a bit about my present, but you will never know my future. This book is the story of how I became a survivor by escaping the war in Liberia and going to the Ivory Coast to live alone without my mother.

While my mother Deborah was being treated badly by our Stepfather AmiShasi in Nigeria, we had to go back to Liberia. Then, escaping another war in Liberia, we went to Nigeria, where I lived with my mother for six months and almost got killed by armed robbers. Ghana was where we lived, in a Liberian refugee camp, and then we returned to Liberia. We escaped yet another war in Liberia and went back to Ghana to live again in the Liberian refugee camp, where we stayed until my family and I came to live in Canada so we could have a good life and a good education.

We were soon to find out that life was not going to be as good as we all dreamed it would be, because after three years of living in Canada, my mother died. Things got harder for me because I became a new mother and I had to learn to take care of a newborn baby all by myself.

Please read this book carefully to understand every character and why they behaved in the ways they did. This book is full of many mixed emotions, so do not be surprised when you find yourself laughing and crying at the same time, even in the same chapter. For me, that was life and I called it normal, the intense feeling of hurt and joy all at the same time.

# CHAPTER 1

# GROWING UP IN LIBERIA

My name is Arnelle; I was born in Monrovia, Liberia, West Africa. I am not sure where to start, but I am going to try my hardest to remember as much as possible. I do not have clear memories about everything that happened in my childhood, but the little I can remember I will share with you.

I remember my sister Yahgahbo and I living alone with our mother Deborah in a townhouse in Liberia. It was in a big compound where other people stayed as well. One morning, we woke up and there was a tall dark-skinned man in the living room wearing my mother's pajamas. My mother said, "This is Mr. AmiShasi; he is my friend."

We greeted him and asked him if he was going to be living with us. My mother replied, saying, "He is only going to stay a little while until he can find his own place, because he has nowhere to stay for now." We started to laugh, because it was very funny to see a man wearing a woman's pajamas. My mother asked what was funny. We told her the reason for our laughter, and she said, "He has no clothes over here, but he is going to go and get them."

After Mr. AmiShasi moved in, we got another big surprise. There was a knock on our door one morning and I opened it to find a white man standing there with a mixed-race kid, so I called my mother. She sent us to our room, but being nosy like kids we wanted to know what was going on, so we left our room door open just a little bit so we could hear.

We overheard the three adults discussing something, but we weren't sure what it was all about. When the man left, we found out that he was the father to our brother. Brother! We did not know we had a brother, but that morning we got the news. Newsflash! My mother called us into the living room where she and Mr. AmiShasi sat with the mixed-race kid. My mother said, "I would like you both to meet your brother Chakakuka, he is going to be staying with us from now on. Be nice to him; he's your older brother, so show him some respect."

I said, "Why no one told us we had a brother?" Mother said it was a long story and she would tell us later. We all went to play, and it turned out to be so much fun to have a brother.

The townhouse only had two bedrooms, so we had to share ours with our brother. One morning, we woke up and said good morning to my mother and Mr. AmiShasi. My mother said to us, "AmiShasi and I would like to have few words with you all, so take a seat in the living room." The three of us sat down awaiting another surprise, and it certainly was.

My mother sat next to Mr. AmiShasi and said, "I need you kids to listen well, because what I am about to tell you all is very important. From now on Mr. AmiShasi is going to be staying over for good. You are to no longer call him Mr. AmiShasi, but Papa." We did not know what to think or say, but the thought of having a father seemed fun, so we all agreed.

Surprise! No, it was not fun, because the man who pretended to be so nice at first came along with many restrictions. We could not eat at a certain time, we had to take a nap at a certain time, and our TV had to be turned off at a certain time. This was not the man we wanted, but my mother was in love with him, so we had to live with his rules. We had friends that lived in the same compound who we would often play with, but our stepfather said we needed to be home at 6 p.m. Also, when they were not home, we had to stay indoors after school and weren't allowed out.

So, when our parents weren't home we opened the house door with the spare key and went out to play with our friends, and when they came home we would run back into the house, shower, and pretend like nothing happened so they would think we'd been good kids all day.

When we went out to play, the neighbours started wondering where our parents were. We would sometimes tell them our parents were asleep and wished not to be disturbed. Those lies did not last too long, because one day one of the neighbour's kids got hurt while we were playing. His parents insisted on speaking to ours, and even though we told them that they were asleep and wished to be left alone, they said they would like to have a few words with them when they woke up. So that evening before our parents got home, we showered and wore our nightgowns and our brother wore his PJs and we pretended nothing happened.

They brought something we liked home from the restaurant for us, but before we could eat it the doorbell rang, and we knew we were in trouble for what happened earlier. Our hearts were pounding faster than a moving train, and when the door opened, there stood our neighbour Helena with a big smile on her face. We were hoping she wasn't going to make comments about what had happened. My mother greeted her, saying, "Hello Helena, what wind brings you to my home this evening? I have been so busy I haven't seen you in a while. Is everything OK?"

Helena said, "No, actually, I came to talk to you about what happened today."

My mother said, "What happened today?"

"The kids were out playing and ours got hurt, and when I wanted to have a word with you, your kids said you were asleep and wished not to be disturbed. So I thought it wise to come later on when you were well rested."

At that point, our hearts dropped. We knew what was about to happen to us, because first we pretended nothing happened then we disrespected orders. My mother told Helena how sorry she was, and that next time when they needed to rest, they would make sure we stayed indoors. Helena said goodbye.

My mother called our stepfather out of their bedroom and told him what happened. She said she was leaving the disciplining to him—big mistake, because we got the whipping of our lives that night. He whipped us so badly, the leather belt he was using was in pieces by the time he was done. He told us to have a shower because we were smelling of spit and sweat. Our whole bodies were covered with bruises and putting water on them made it hurt even more.

We did not get the food they brought for us because they said we did not listen. I was sorry for what happened to us, but I felt even sorrier for Chakakuka, because he is mixed-race and you could really see the red marks all over him. School was closed for the summer, so that made it even worse, because when our parents went out they locked us up in the house and took the key with them. All that was left was our bedroom window to chat with our friends.

That was the only way they could visit us and the only way we could communicate with them. The window wasn't big enough, so most of the time we found ourselves fighting over who was going to get the better spot to look outside and chat with our friends. Being alone at home made us so bored; we did not know what to do, so our friends started bringing us stuff like candy that their parents gave them. There was no way of getting it, so we decided to make a hole in the window screen. We thought we were the smartest kids ever until we found out that we'd just cost ourselves more trouble. Each time we took stuff from our friends, the hole in the window got bigger, which allowed more mosquitoes into our house.

It became a concern to my mother, because it seemed that each time she used the mosquito spray, more mosquitoes came into the house. She decided to find where they were coming from. She checked the whole house, and when she got to our room, we heard her scream. She yelled for us to come and see what we had done. We knew it was going to come to this, but we were not sure how long it was going take for my mother to find out.

None of us wanted to be the first to enter the room. We heard her scream again, "You guys better get in here very fast, because when I reach out there to get you, you won't find this funny at all." We had no choice but to enter the room together. She called us one at a time to the window to show us what we had done. She said, "Do you know how expensive these things were? You are all spoiled and do not even care, right?" We stood there with no answer, because we knew what we had done was wrong. But at the time we did it, it was our only way of connecting with the outside world.

She said to us, "I am going call your father to see this." She called, "AmiShasi, come see what the children did."

Mr. AmiShasi entered the room and saw what we did, and said, "So, this is what you people have done, right? Go into the living room and I am going to teach you a lesson." Silly us, we were so happy when we heard him say "teach us a lesson." We thought he was going to help us with our schoolwork, but we saw him come out of their room with his leather belt in his hand, and he told us to stand in a line. We got the beating of our lives while our mom stood there and did not tell him to stop.

To her we were just getting discipline. But we asked ourselves how she could stand there and watch while he beat us like that. We started to hate Mr. AmiShasi now; he was always beating us.

That day went by, and we continued with our day-to-day life. One evening, while we were watching movies as a family in the living room, Mr. AmiShasi told my mother that he would be right back. She said OK, and when he returned, he had a big smile on his face.

He had a surprise for her and told us to close our eyes, and that my mother should close her eyes, too. We closed our eyes and held hands while he led us outside. He said to my mother, "Happy birthday!" She opened her eyes to see a brand-new BMW. He had bought it for her birthday present, and even being that young I knew it was a very sweet thing to do, because at the time I did not know the word romantic or what it meant.

She screamed and gave him a big hug and a kiss, and he suggested we all take a drive in it. But at that time, my mother didn't know how to drive, so he drove her instead and promised he was going to teach her how to drive. We then thought that this man was not bad after all, so we started to like him. Although he liked his intense discipline, we still thought it would be nice having him as a father. After a few days, my mother got our window screen fixed and there were no more mosquitoes. Each evening, she would use Spray Gone and we would all go sit outside and wait for a few hours until it was safe to go back inside.

We learned the sound of the BMW because the house was up on a hill, so when our parents were on their way home, we would run in the house and behave as if we had been good all day. We made sure not to cause any trouble while we were out playing so our parents would not get complaints about us and learn what we had been up to. I know you might be wondering how we were able to go outside, since our parents always locked the doors before leaving for work. One morning, when our mom and dad were getting ready for work, we distracted them and took the spare key. That is why we behaved so well when we went out to play, because if we got in trouble and it got back to our parents, we would be in bigger trouble than ever.

Things at home were good. Each day, before my mother went to work, she would cook food for us and put it in a bowl, with different colours for each of us, but we didn't have much of an appetite. We wanted anything that was sweet in the house, like chocolate, candy—you name it. My mother noticed something was wrong, because each time she got home from work our food would be untouched.

She called us into the kitchen and asked why we did not eat the food she took her time to cook. One of us would say they did not like it, the next said it was too spicy, and the other said it was not their favourite. My mother now had to make three different meals before going to work, and still the same thing happened when she got home. She went out and got us vitamins, thinking maybe that was the problem, but we still didn't want to eat.

When she checked around the kitchen to find out what was wrong, she realized that all the sweets in the house were gone. She called our stepdad and we had a little family meeting. They said that from then on, they would need to lock up all the sweets in the house and would only give them to us if we did good things.

All the sweets were put away, but our parents made one mistake: they left the cookie jar high up on the top of the shelves. So, when they left for work, we got together as a team and planned how we were going to get the cookies down. It sounded like so much fun, so we decided to form a human ladder. Chakakuka was at the bottom, I stood on his shoulders, and Yahgahbo stood on mine, but the human ladder was not strong enough.

When Yahgahbo was passing the stuff down from up above, she slipped, and I slipped, and we all came tumbling down on the big bag of rice, and the rice in the bag spilled all over the kitchen floor. We were in panic, and before we could clean it our parents got home. That's when they realized that beating us wasn't going to change anything, it was just going to get us to make more trouble. They both decided to try a different method of discipline: we were not allowed to watch television that evening. They needed to figure out what to do about us being destructive. Our stepfather was not happy about what happened at all.

He was so upset, he decided that my mother would not use the remaining rice in the bag. She called some guys that lived in the neighbourhood over and told them they could have it. Those guys were so happy it felt like

Christmas for them. They told my mother thanks and promised to come and help her out with some housework if she needed the help, which she and our stepfather agreed to.

I'm not sure what happened, but one day one of the guys decided that he would disrespect and challenge our stepfather to a fight. I prayed that guy would not challenge our stepfather, but he did, because he saw that he was skinny. He overlooked the strength of Mr. AmiShasi.

Our stepfather got very mad and promised to teach the guy a lesson. We knew what he meant when he talked about teaching someone a lesson, because we had been taught by him. We knew the guy was in for some big trouble, but we did not know how big his trouble was going to be until it happened.

My mother tried to stop him from going out to fight this guy, but our father said if he did not teach this guy a lesson, he would think that one day he could come back and disrespect or take advantage of our family.

Our stepfather came outside and didn't say a single word. He watched as the guy carried on talking and saying stuff. Mr. AmiShasi just walked to him, gave him one punch, and he was on the ground. Then Mr. AmiShasi, with the wooden slippers he was wearing, stepped on the guy's mouth and broke his front tooth.

People came running to stop the fight, but before they could get there the fight was over. They had to rush the guy to the hospital, and since that day everyone became scared of how strong Mr. AmiShasi was, and no one ever brought disrespect to our family again.

Our stepfather told my mother to tell the other guys that we wouldn't be needing their help anymore. He told her he was going to send for his sister Emelia from Nigeria to help them out for a bit with disciplining us, so that we could learn to behave ourselves. My mother thought that was a great idea.

# CHAPTER 2

# OUR DRUNKEN EXPERIENCE & LIVING WITH A NEW AUNTY

Our stepfather had a habit of letting us taste his drinks whenever he was drinking; my mother tried many times to warn him, saying it wasn't good to give kids alcohol, but he never listened. One day my mother was away, and I remember our stepfather was in the living room drinking. He called us over, and said, "Girls, come have a taste." My sister Yahgahbo and I asked him what it was he was drinking, and he said chocolate milk.

It was not chocolate milk he was drinking, it was Baileys Irish Cream. However, because we were young, could not read, and did not know what it was, we believed that it was chocolate milk, so we both had a taste of it. It tasted good, but it was strong. We asked for more, but he said, "No, I am not giving you kids no more of this stuff. It is not too good for kids."

Just then, the next-door neighbour—we called him George—came over and told our stepfather that he had some strong alcohol called London dry gin, so our stepfather forgot the large bottle of Baileys on the bedroom floor. While my sister and I were watching cartoons, we both saw the large bottle, and I said, "Isn't that the chocolate milk that Papa left on the floor?"

We got down from the bed, took the large bottle of Baileys, and drank the whole thing. We got so drunk we both almost died from alcohol poisoning. Meanwhile, our stepfather was sitting next door and did not know what was going on in his home. The whole house was a big mess, because Yahgahbo and I took the food my mother made and spilled it everywhere, plus there was vomit all over the house.

After throwing up and making a mess, we went back into our parents' bedroom and sat on the bed to watch cartoons, but because we were so drunk the cartoons were even more funny to us and we couldn't get ourselves to stop laughing. My mother got home and started screaming, because there was vomit and food mess everywhere. She heard us laughing non-stop from her bedroom and wondered what was going on. She opened their bedroom door to find us drunk.

She called our names and we did not respond, just kept laughing, so she turned off the TV to see if that would make us stop, but it did not. She saw the large empty bottle of Baileys, so she knew we were drunk. She got so mad at our stepfather—first for letting us have a taste of his drink and then forgetting the bottle on the floor, making it easy for us to get our hands on it.

She screamed his name out the door, because he was still at the neighbour's house drinking. "AmiShasi, come here and see what you have done to the children, they are about to die!" said my mother, then she started crying. He quickly ran in, very confused, and did not know what they should do, so he suggested that they give us a cold bath and glass of milk.

My mother was so mad, she did not know what to do; she wanted to beat us for drinking, but our stepfather said that if she did we would die for sure. She undressed us, put Yahgahbo and me in the tub, and poured cold water on our heads. After that, they put our nightgowns on us and gave us a glass of milk, and off to bed we went. The next day, we slept all day because we felt so sick, and we could not eat anything but soup. My mother explained to us what had happened and told us to never let it happen again. She also gave our stepfather a very strong warning and told him he should never give us any of his alcohol to taste again.

He agreed, because he saw what giving us alcohol did and how we almost died. We were causing so much trouble for our parents that finally their solution arrived: it was our father's sister Emelia who came all the way from Nigeria to give us her own kind of discipline. Our parents said to us, "Your Aunty Emelia is going to stay here until your school opens." We introduced ourselves to her and she told us that we could call her

Aunty Emelia, so we said OK, and away we went. We were happy that she came to stay with us, but we were happier to find out how much good stuff she brought: some Gari, dried Cayenne pepper, some dried fish, dried shrimps, palm oil… The list goes on and on, but the things she brought were very nice.

We did not want anything to do with the other stuff she brought; our main interest was in those big dried shrimps. She brought them for my mother and to cook some traditional African soup with it, but we thought it would be something nice to snack on, so we ended up eating almost every bit of them.

When she woke up to check on the dried shrimps she had left outside on the mat to dry, she discovered that they were almost gone and she knew no one could have taken them but us. She called us and asked what happened to her shrimps, and we said we knew nothing about it, and maybe someone took them because she left them outside. Out of frustration, she sent us all to our room and told us to go to bed, and that she didn't want to hear one sound from us. We obeyed and off to our room we went, but did we keep quiet? No, we didn't; instead, we whispered to each other and laughed silently. Each time we heard her footsteps coming toward our bedroom door, we would close our eyes and pretend to be asleep.

She knew we were pretending to be asleep, but she was determined to catch us in the act of pretending, so she walked away so we could hear her footsteps leave, then she crept back to our bedroom door to listen. We thought she was gone, but what we did not know was that all along she stood next to our bedroom door listening to us talk. Then our bedroom door opened, and it was too late for us to pretend because we were caught in the act. She said to us, "Every one of you wake up right now and pump tire." I know you are wondering what "pump tire" means; well, it means you hold your ears and repeatedly bounce up and down on your feet until you cannot do it anymore.

We did that repeatedly until our feet started to give up on us. She told us we were going to do that for an hour while she slept. That made us so angry that we did not like her very much, but we did not know that it was just the beginning of our discipline. She tried cooking for us, but we did not like her cooking, so before my mother left for work, she cooked our meal and we all had our own bowl.

When my mother left for work, our aunty took our food and told us that we would only play in it because we were not hungry. She told us that when we ready to eat, we should come and ask her, and she would know if we were hungry or not. We waited and waited and got so hungry we decided to ask her for our food, but she refused and said we were not that hungry yet and that she was busy having her nap and wished not to be disturbed.

As always, we came up with a plan to be the Three Ninjas. Since our sister Yahgahbo was the smaller one, she would go in first, then I would go second, and our brother would go third. We all made it into the kitchen, ate as much food as possible, and decided to return to our bedroom. On our way back, we heard sound coming from the washroom; the only person who could be using the washroom was Aunty Emelia. Therefore, we had to be very careful about our return from the kitchen, because if she caught us we were going to get some real discipline.

Yahgahbo went in first and then I followed, but when it was Chakakuka's turn to follow, our aunty Emelia caught him trying to enter the bedroom. She said to him, "Do not dare take another step! Now you will tell me where you were coming from." He replied, saying "nowhere," and then she said to him, "If you are coming from nowhere, then why does it look like you were going somewhere?"

She then said to him, "Follow me into the kitchen, because I want to make sure you did not touch the food I told you not to touch." Upon arriving in the kitchen, she saw that all three meals where tampered with, so she turned to Chakakuka and said, "Who touched this food?" Chakakuka told her he was not the only one and that my sister and I were a part of what happened.

She did not believe him, so she said, "I am taking you to the room so we can check on them, and if I find them sleeping you are in big trouble with me." We heard them walking toward our room, so we closed our eyes and pretended to be sleeping. When she opened the door, she said to him, "These girls are fast asleep, so why were you saying they were with you when the food got touched?" When he tried to explain, she said to him, "Not another word from you. Now, start pushing the wall and make sure to push it until it breaks." You might be wondering what "push the wall until it breaks" means. Well, it means for one to stand facing the wall with their feet all the way behind them as if they were tipping toes, lean forward with both hands on the wall with arms stretched wide and fingers spread apart, and push the wall with the intention of breaking it. But we are all aware that no one is strong enough to push the wall of a house until it breaks.

After his punishment, he was mad about our aunty catching him but not catching us, too. However, it was not our fault; he should have been faster and smarter. She came with her own rules that we had to live by; they were so intense it still affects us today. She said we were not allowed to eat and drink water at the same time, because the water takes up a lot of room in our stomach and we would not have space left for food. When we ate, we ate all the meat off our plate, and once the meat was gone we were done with the food, so she told us we would have to eat up the rest of our food before we could eat the meat.

If you ever see me eat all my food but forget about eating the meat, it is because of what I have been used to growing up. Her intense training was becoming very effective, and things started to go very well. Our parents were very pleased about what they saw but were not sure if it was going to last for long.

When our parents were sure that her training and discipline were working, it was time for Aunty Emelia to return to Nigeria. Although we could not stand her, we started missing her immediately, because secretly she became our friend, someone who was always around to make sure we were doing the right things and to make sure we learned from what we were being taught. In many ways, she was a nice woman.

# Chapter 3

# The Night We Did Not Fall Asleep

Our stepdad's sister left for Nigeria, so again we had the house all to ourselves, and we were so happy about it. We still forgot the rules about not staying up late at night to watch movies, and that night there were some scary movies on TV and we wanted to watch them. We thought our parents were asleep, so we started to watch; each time one of our parents' woke to use the washroom we pretended to be asleep.

Our stepfather noticed that we weren't sleeping. He pretended that he didn't know what was going on and waited till we got comfortable. We thought we had made sure that they were sleeping, and we crept to our room and started enjoying the scary movie.

Our movie ended when we discovered Mr. AmiShasi standing there watching us watch the scary movie. The moment we noticed him, we tried to pretend to be asleep, but it was too late for us—we were already caught. He said to us, "Now, I know very well that you kids are not asleep, so you all get up and go into our bedroom."

How we wished that we had gone to bed early that night instead of disobeying our parents. We walked into our parents' room and our stepdad said to us, "I will show you kids how disrespectful I can be. You kids will pump tire, and after that you kids will push the wall of our bedroom until it breaks."

We all knew that, little as we were, it would be impossible to break the wall just by pushing it. He made us push that wall all night while they slept. Early the next morning, he woke and told us we could go to our bedroom and sleep.

We were like robots; we could not move our legs and it was very difficult for us to walk, but we made it back to our room, so very angry with our stepfather. We were very sure we learned our lesson, because we never repeated what we did that night.

In the morning, we had to apologize to our parents for what we did the night before and promise never to repeat it. Our apologies were accepted and everything and everyone around us seemed OK, until one day we got news that would change our lives forever. From that day, things were never the same, and that day determined our future.

As a child, you really do not worry much about what is going on around you, because you know your parents are there to fix things and make them better.

# CHAPTER 4

# THE WAR CHANGED OUR LIVES

It was very early in the morning, when all of a sudden there was a loud pounding on our door, so our parents woke to see what was going on. They opened the door to see some of the boys in the area whom our parents had helped before. My mother Deborah asked the boys what happened to bring them to our house this early and knock on our door so loud.

The boys told my mother that they needed to remove us from the house and take us somewhere for safety, because by the late evening the rebels would capture the entire area. If we stay, no one is going to survive. Our stepfather said it was a joke and that it could not be possible, and that the boys were telling a lie so they could come over to our home and steal everything after we were all gone. My mother screamed at him, saying that from what she saw, he was only concerned about material things and that he had no value for his life or ours.

She told him he could stay if he so chooses and protect the material things, but she was getting her children out of there and to safety. He said to her, "Fine, I will stay, and if it is true what these boys are saying I will follow when you and the kids leave." My mother then asked the boys when they would come and get us from the house, and the boys said they should return with a car in an hour's time. My mother then asked the boys why they were certain all of this was going to happen.

The boys told her that secretly they were fighters and they were informed about this, and because she had been so kind to their families by giving them food and making sure they were OK, they could not just sit there and allow something bad to happen to us. My mother started to give Jehovah God thanks for sending us a miracle. After the boys left, my mother turned to our stepfather and said, "You see how it pays to be kind to people? What if we been unkind to these boys? They would have left us here to be killed or they would have killed us themselves." She then said to him, "You sure you would not like to come with us?"

He replied to her by saying no, that he was man enough to take care of himself and that he would come after. She said OK and came to our room, told us that something bad was about to happen, and that she was taking us somewhere where we would all be safe. She also told us our stepfather would come later on because he had a few things he wanted to take care of before he left. She started to pack things that we may need; we did not even get a chance to shower or eat something because the boys were back in no time to take us to safety.

They arrived in a pickup truck; there were already other people sitting in the back with guns, and the boys we knew to be nice were all dressed up like bad people with fabrics around their heads and guns in their hands as well. My mother told us not to be worried, that everything was going to be OK, and that we were safe and going somewhere the bad people who hurt and kill innocent people would not harm us. We gave our stepfather big hugs and kisses and he promised to see us very soon, so we said OK and got in the pickup truck with my mother, and off we went.

While driving in the pickup, we saw many people in a panic with their things in bundles tied up on their heads, walking along the roads in large groups. I guess we were all heading to the same place, a place of safety. We arrived at a badlooking area that was a safe place and were told that we would be OK for now until things got a bit better. Before the boys left, my mother called them all together and begged them to please look after our dad and make sure he was safe until he was ready to leave, and then asked them to bring him to us.

We ended up in a tiny little room; it was in a big house with a lot of bedrooms and each family had one. The kitchen and bathroom were shared, and all of the kids played outside together. In the house we saw that most of the kids ate together from one large bowl, but my mother always made sure there was food for us to eat. When it was time for us to eat, she brought us into the room and fed us.

Our stepfather returned, and for us that was good news because he was OK and nothing bad happened to him, but he had a lot of stories from where we last stayed. He told my mother that everything the boys said was true. He said that when we left that day, the rebels captured the entire area that evening and our next-door neighbour George was scared because the rebels were looking for men and killing them, so George climbed up into the ceiling and hid there. The rebels entered George's house, asking his wife who all was at home, and she tells them it was just her and the kids. They asked if she was sure she was not keeping government soldiers in her house and she told them yes, but because George was so fat, when the rebels were about to leave the house, he fell out of the ceiling flat onto the ground.

Even the rebels were scared, because the noise was too loud and the fall left a very large hole in the ceiling. The rebels jumped out of fear, furiously looked at George's wife and said to her, "We thought you told us it was just you and the kids? Now where is this man coming from and who is he?"

She said, "He is my husband; he was hiding in the ceiling because he heard you people were killing men." The rebels took a long look at George. There was nothing they could do with him, because he was too fat for them to ask him to fight alongside them and the look on his face showed that he needed them to have mercy on him or else fear alone would kill him.

Our stepfather told my mother that it was odd that the rebels did nothing to them, but instead warned them to leave because the other rebels were not as nice as they were. Before the rebels left, George opened a very large drink and said, "I need to celebrate my life because I almost got killed today, but all praise be to God that I am still standing." Our stepfather said that they had a lot of fun drinking with the rebels and they even helped him transport all our things somewhere safe so that no one could try to steal them.

He told my mother that the group he met were nice people. The rebels also said that they could help George's family to safety if he wanted them to, and George gladly accepted because of his fear of what happened earlier, and he worried that if he ended up in the wrong hands he might not be so lucky again.

Our stepfather said the rebels gave him a ride along with the boys my mother knew. He said many people left the area and it was like a ghost town, but he was glad that he was able to get everything out of there. My mother Deborah was glad that he was safe, and we were glad he was safe as well.

When things started getting back to normal, our parents had to get someone to look after us while they made some arrangements of where we going to stay, so my mother found a Bassa girl called Zoegoh and she was to be kind of like a nanny. My mother brought her to the house so she could clean, cook, and make sure everything was OK with us. When our parents left the house, Zoegoh did her own thing, like leaving us to play without any supervision, and when she knew our parents were almost home, she would call us to give us a shower and get us ready for bed.

I have always been the wild one amongst my siblings, so one day when she was not paying attention to us, I was playing running race with the boys and into the cement blocks my leg went. I hurt myself really badly and could not walk. Upon hearing what happened in our parent's absence, my mother got mad at Zoegoh and said if she was paying attention this would not have happened. My mother was very mad that I did not heed the warnings about playing wild. I promised to take very good care of my wound, and she said that when she was finished with me I would not be such a tomboy again.

The next morning it was treatment time for my wound, and it was one of the days in my life I will never forget. My mother took a bucket half full of boiled water and only added two to three cups of cold water to it, but that did not help because the water was so hot I could feel my soul being boiled as well. I screamed hard and loud for someone to help me escape from the pain, but all I heard was my mother telling me to tell myself that there is no pain and that the pain would go away. She also said to me that this would be a lesson learned for me to stop being such a tomboy.

I could not stop crying; in my scream I yelled everyone's name out for help, including my own, that was how much I could not think anymore.

After many painful treatments over a week or two, my wound started to heal and I became a bit more careful as to how I played with my friends, because I knew what getting hurt meant for me. Because of what happened to me, our nanny Zoegoh had to give an account every day when our parents got home about what she did all day to make sure she took care of us. Even after she admitted the things she did all day, our parents would still call us to confirm that what she said was true.

I'm not sure what happened, but my mother noticed our nanny Zoegoh and it was not good at all. Apparently, Zoegoh had been having a hidden relationship with some guy in the area that our parents were unaware of, and that is why she had not been paying us much attention. The night my mother caught Zoegoh was a night Zoegoh wished didn't happen.

From what we heard, Zoegoh was busy having sex with the guy at night not far from our house in an open field, and when she was caught my mother got so furious she almost killed the girl with a beating. Zoegoh was in her teens, fifteen or sixteen, when this all happened, and my mother was scared that Zoegoh could get herself pregnant by the wrong person and end up a single mother. So, all night my mother beat Zoegoh and that night our stepfather beat the guy up very badly for having a sexual relationship with an underage girl.

That night our stepfather begged my mother to allow Zoegoh in the house to sleep, but she refused and said that Zoegoh would sleep outside, and by the morning she would continue her discipline with Zoegoh. The next time, Zoegoh would think before having sex with a guy who knew she was underage.

The next morning my mother continued her beating of Zoegoh. It was intense by the morning, because my mother, after beating Zoegoh up, rubbed her entire body with cayenne pepper, including her private parts and her eyes, and put her completely naked in the sun to sit all day. Our stepfather came home, saw what happened, got very mad at my mother, and said that what she was doing was too much and that it needed to stop.

He went out, took Zoegoh out of the sun, gave her water to wash her eyes, and told her to shower and put on some clean clothes. When my mother learned what happened, she got mad at our stepfather and it ended up in a fight. The next day when they left the house, Zoegoh ran away and we never saw her again. When our parents returned and Zoegoh was nowhere to be found, our stepfather said to my mother, "You see why I was telling you to take it easy on her and just talk to her? Now that she has gone, what would you do if something bad happens to her?"

My mother said that she would come back, but they waited for many days and there was no Zoegoh, so my mother gave up waiting. The war slowed a little and things went back to normal a bit, so our parents found a place for us to stay that we could call our own. We made new friends and had a new environment. The people around us seemed very friendly and everyone was like one big family.

There was this girl name Talena, and when we were all settled in, she came over to ask if my sister Yahgahbo and I were interested in playing with her and her friends, so we agreed and went out to play. We became friends and I got to meet her mom, dad, brothers, and sisters.

She was the smallest in her house, the last for her parents, and all her older brothers and sisters took turns taking care of her, making sure that she was OK. Every now and then they would call out to make sure she was at the neighbour's house, and if they didn't hear from her or see her they came looking for her. One time we were playing, and her mom called her to go home to eat but she said she was not yet ready, that she was still playing, so she did not answer.

Her mom sent one of her older sisters to look for her. When she heard her sister calling, we started running to hide from her. Her sister searched everywhere and could not find us, so she returned home. After we ran around the community and played for a bit, she got really hungry and decided to return home. She asked if I would like to come along, but I told her that I had to go home as well because by now my mother would be looking for me. She said OK, and we made plans to meet the next day to play.

My mother Deborah had my brother, sister, and I register in the same school as Talena; I got excited because I wouldn't have to be just the new girl at school but a new girl who already had a friend there. We started school, and in no time I started to know my way around and make other new friends. During lunchtime at school, we all played together, and after school, her brother or sister would come and pick her up. We had my mother to come and get us.

I'm not sure what happened, but one day Talena fell sick and wished to not talk to anyone, so her mom sent for me. When I came over, her mom said, "My daughter is not feeling so well, and she asked that I send for you to keep her company."

When she saw me, she perked up and started talking, and her mom was surprised to see her being a bit active. Her mom saw the opportunity to ask her to have some food. Talena's mother even gave me some food to eat. When she saw me eating, she took her spoon and tried to feed herself. It was hard for her because she had no appetite, but she wanted to try. Talena managed to eat just a little bit of her food and then she did not want anymore.

Her mother told her it was nice to see her try, and that if she kept trying to eat every day, she would start feeling well enough to go out and play with all her friends. My mother kind of knew that I might be at my friend Talena's house, but she needed to be sure so she started to call out for me to come home. Hearing my mother calling me, I told Talena's mother that I had to return home but that I would be back to check on Talena to make sure she was OK.

I said goodbye to Talena and promised that I would be back to check on her to make sure that she was getting well. After my goodbyes, I quickly returned home to find out why my mother had called out for me. When I got home, my mother said, "Where have you been?" I told her that I was at Talena's house visiting and that she was not feeling well. My mother asked what happened to Talena; I told her that I wasn't sure, but that she might have malaria.

After about a week, Talena started to feel a lot better, so she came over to my house to play, and when my mother was done cooking, we all ate and then we went out to play again. When it was time for her to go home, I walked her to her house. Her mom was done cooking and asked if we wanted something to eat. We said yes and were given something to eat, and later had the chance to go out to play some more. It was getting dark, so her mom asked one of her big sisters to give us all a shower.

We did not bring a change of clothes with us, so her big sister suggested that after we showered, we could go home and change into our nightgowns and that our brother could wear his PJs. Her sister showered all the girls together in the big tub and then showered our brother Chakakuka separately. When we got home, my mother was thankful that we had taken a shower, and she sent us to our bedroom to get changed.

We all became so close that when her parents did not see her, they knew she was over at my house and if our parents did not see us, they knew we were over at Talena's house.

One night our parents went out. I'm not sure if it was to a party, but they went out somewhere and they took ever so long to get there. They asked some guy who they only kind of knew to stay at the house with us until they returned, so when it was late, Yahgahbo and I put on our nightgowns and Chakakuka put on his PJs and the guy sat us outside and told us funny stories. Chakakuka and Yahgahbo got tired of waiting for our parents to return, so off to bed they went. I was worried about what had happened to them, so I decided to stay up late and wait while the guy kept telling me funny stories.

When our parents returned, they were very concerned about why I was up so late sitting alone with the guy. I told them I was worried about them and I did not want to sleep until they returned. My stepfather got mad; he did not trust the guy, so he shouted at him and told him to leave and never come back to the house. But before they let him go, they decided to check me to make sure I was not sexually abused by him. I was so confused and did not know what was going on. All I remember was my parents taking me inside the house, getting a flashlight, pulling down my panties, and checking between my legs.

I was not sure what they were looking for, so I became very shy because my mother was not the only one checking me, she was with my stepfather. I did not like that at all, but who was I to say? They let the guy go after finding out that I was OK and that nothing had happened to me.

I am not sure after what had happened that I would ever be OK, because I kept wondering what would make them do that, but now that I am old enough to know that the world is not so very nice a place, I understand why they thought that way. But what I will never understand is why my mother allowed my stepfather to look between my legs at my private parts. My mother was always very careful with us and concerned with who we were around, because she did not want to see any of us get hurt sexually. She made sure to check where we were all the time and told us to always come and check at home so that she knew we were safe.

My birthday came and I didn't know that our parents had a surprise for me. On my birthday, my mother cooked lots of food. She made popcorn in bags with candy in it for all of my friends. There was jollof rice, potato salad, fried chicken and cake. During the party, our parents brought out my surprise birthday present: my very own bicycle. I was very excited.

I could not wait to get on it. Both my parents helped me get on my bicycle and taught me how to ride it. It had training wheels on it and that made it a bit easier to ride. Our friends got excited about my bicycle, too, and they chased me for a chance to be the next person to ride it when I come to a stop. Each day after I woke up, ate, and took a bath, I took my bicycle for a ride in the neighbourhood.

My friends were always taking turns riding my bike, including Chakakuka and Yahgahbo. Talena got mad because my other friends were not allowing her to ride my bicycle, so she came to complain and I told them that if any of them take too long with the bicycle, they would not be allowed to ride again.

Just when we were getting adjusted to where we lived, something happened. One evening there was shooting, and we all had to stay indoors until we heard that it was safe to go out.

At home, everyone was glued to their radio listening for information about where the rebels were and how close they were getting to where we were staying. Everyone got very scared, and within days the shooting was getting near, so our parents started to pack up our things. They were not waiting for things to get bad, they were ready to leave. There was no going out to play with our friends and there was no going to school. People started leaving the neighbourhood one at a time, making the place really quiet.

My parents, on the other hand, were making arrangements for us to leave. My parents had a talk with Talena's parents, and they were planning on leaving soon as well. They had big sons and daughters and they did not want to risk their kids getting discovered by the rebels. All arrangements for us to leave had been made and it was just a matter of time before we left. We lived at that neighbourhood for a little bit and then we had to move to a place called Jamaica Road.

Before leaving, I asked my parents if it would be OK if we went over to Talena and her parents' house to say goodbye, and my parents agreed. We went over, visited for a bit, and my parents told them that they had found a safe place for us to go. When asked where they would stay, Talena's family said they planned to live with a member of their family in a safe environment for the moment.

# CHAPTER 5
# JAMAICA ROAD

Bags packed, house packed, and off to our new safe location we went. After saying our goodbyes, we got in the car and drove to Jamaica Road, a place in Monrovia, Liberia. I do not think I had any expectation of how the place would look, I only wanted to be safe. We drove for a bit and then came to a stop at a house on Jamaica Road located not far from a big cotton tree; at least, that is what the locals called the tree.

At the house lived other people, and they were excited to see us. I'm not sure how our stepfather found that place, but he definitely knew his way around. People at the house came running to help us get our things in the house. Most of the things our stepfather took down from the car were our clothes and food. He told my mother Deborah that he would find a place to put the rest and she agreed, because we only had one room in the house for all five of us.

We moved in and our stepfather took our things to one of his Lebanese friend's place for safe keeping. I'm not sure how many rooms were in that house, but it was a lot and each family only had one bedroom to stay with their family, except for an old man who lived in a room by himself. We got settled in, but as kids we wanted to be out playing. My mother told us that we had to make sure that we were playing right in front of the house. We agreed, and went out to play with the other kids from the family who shared the house with us. We did not have any particular friends at that moment, we just wanted to play.

My mother told us that our grandmother Stuciah lived not far from where we stayed, but we were not allowed to look for her because the roads were not safe. The first time my mother cooked at the new house, she put our food in a big dish and allowed us to eat outside. The next thing we knew, other kids joined us and started eating our food, so we did not have much to eat. My mother suggested that it was not a good idea for us to eat outside anymore, because we did not have much food and we had to manage what we had.

There was news that the rebels were killing foreigners, so our stepfather had to leave Liberia for a bit and return when it was safe to do so. Before he left, he made sure my mother took enough food from his Lebanese friend's supermarket to last us for a year. My mother had so much food stacked up in the room that we were not allowed to tell anyone about it, because people would come and kill you for your food and steal it.

I'm not sure where Chakakuka found a friend, but he met a mixed-race boy named Jason who lived right next to the big cotton tree. The boy's mother was African and his father was European, and the house had a fenced yard. The boy had three sisters, and I became friends with one of them. Her name was Tatilia, and she was the nicer among her sisters, who were a bit selfish and refused to play with other kids, but when they saw their sister Tatilia and me being good friends, they slowly started to come around a little.

Chakakuka loved having this new friend of his, but my brother's main interest in him was the fact that his mother cooked on time and my brother got to eat with him. Chakakuka told Jason they should share food.

"When your mother cooks, you and I will eat your food, and when my mother cooks, you and I will eat my food," he suggested, so the boy agreed. As for my friend Tatilia, she would sometimes invite me to eat and I would tell her no thanks, and sometimes when it was time for them to eat, she told me that she would be back after she had eaten.

I know you are probably wondering why we were out playing at our friend's place when a war was going on. Well, Jamaica Road was safe for a while; the rebels had not yet reached it. Every day, people listened to their radio to monitor the rebel's location. One day we tried figuring out the way to our grandmother Stuciah's house, but we got lost so we came running back home. We did not tell my mother about it because she would have been really mad.

Chakakuka was over at Jason's place almost all the time. Every time my mother asked for him, he was at his friend's place. One day my mother sent for him, and when he returned, he was like, "We were almost about to eat but then you sent for me to come home." My mother said, "I thought I told you guys not to eat from strangers." Chakakuka said, "Well, the boy is my friend and we both agreed to share food." My mother said, "Food is so hard to get. What if the boy's parents do not cook, or what if we do not cook?" Chakakuka said, "Well, if they don't cook, he would not get to eat any of my food."

While my brother was interested in Jason's mom's cooking, I was interested in being friends with his sister Tatilia. Tatilia was always so nice to me but her sisters were selfish, and when Tatilia called them so we could all play together, they would say they were not interested in playing with us and the both of them would play by themselves.

One day while at home, Tatilia called for us to go and play at her house. My mother was at home and said that I had to take Yahgahbo along with me to play, and if I refused, I may as well stay home. I agreed to take Yahgahbo with me. We arrived at Tatilia's place and her sisters were outside playing, and when they saw us, they decided to continue playing and behave as though we were not there.

Later, when they saw that we were playing and having lots of fun, they slowly started to come around, and next thing we knew, they were having fun running around with us and playing. After their mother was done cooking, they invited us to eat with them, but we told them no thanks and home we went.

Chakakuka and Jason returned to our home one day when my mother was almost done cooking. As soon as Chakakuka realized the food was almost ready to eat, he pretended that he wasn't feeling well, so my mother told him to go and lay down and said that she would give him some medication later. Jason waited around, hoping to eat some of the food my mother cooked, but our mother told the boy that it was time to go home because it was getting late.

Jason left to go home, and not long after he left, Chakakuka said he was not feeling sick anymore and was well enough to eat. He ate his food alone with a great deal of satisfaction and pretended as though he did not have an agreement with Jason for them to share food. My mother noticed that Chakakuka was feeling well immediately after Jason left to go home, so she asked him, "I thought you said you were not well when your friend came to visit you." Chakakuka replied that he was now feeling better.

I'm not sure what happened, but one day when Chakakuka returned from Jason's place, he told my mother that when Jason asked for him, she should tell him that he was not home. My mother said to Chakakuka, "Why should I lie for you when I know very well that you're home?" Chakakuka said, "Just say it and I will explain to you later. I know what I am talking about."

My mother asked Chakakuka, "What is going on between you and your friend? The last time the kid was here to visit you, you pretended to be sick." Chakakuka said that nothing was going on and that they were still friends. I told mother that Chakakuka was hiding from his friend because he did not want him to eat his food after eating his friend's food. My mother said to Chakakuka, "That is very bad behaviour, and I will not entertain it from you."

My mother said to Chakakuka, "When your friend gets here you better go out to play with him, and when I am done cooking the both of you will eat your food together." Jason came to visit Chakakuka, but he refused to come out of the room. My mother said to the boy, "Chakakuka is refusing to come out of the room to play." Jason was about to leave when my mother Deborah told him, "I am almost done cooking, so I want you to wait so you can have something to eat."

Jason said OK and waited for my mother to finish her cooking. Meanwhile, Chakakuka heard everything and thought that my mother was going to give Jason food to eat and later he would get to eat his own food all by himself, but little did he know that the food the boy was going to eat was going to be Chakakuka's food. My mother finished with her cooking and gave Jason Chakakuka's food to eat. After he ate, he said thanks and left to go home. After the boy left, Chakakuka came out of the room.

Chakakuka said, "What is that boy's problem? Why did he take so long to leave?" He asked our mother, "Did you give him food to eat?" My mother responded by saying, "Yes, I gave him food to eat, and it was your food so forget about eating today." Chakakuka got very mad and said, "But Mama, why did you do that! I did not instruct you to give my food to him; you did not even ask me, you just gave him my food."

My mother asked Chakakuka, "Did you eat today at his house when you visited him?" Chakakuka said yes, that he had eaten at his friend's house, but the food was not enough and that his friend ate most of it. My mother said, "Well, that is none of my business. If you do not want anyone eating your food do not go and eat someone else's. Today this nonsense is going to stop. From now on you are not allowed to go over to your friend's house to eat his food and he is not allowed to come over here to eat your food. So tomorrow, you go and tell your friend that the both of you can no longer share food. I see this being a big problem if you do not put a stop to this. This should teach you a lesson that if you are not willing to share, do not go and share what others have." So Chakakuka went to sleep hungry.

The next day came and Jason came over to play, but Chakakuka was still mad at him for eating his food the day before. Chakakuka said to Jason, "Why did you eat my food yesterday?" The boy said, "But you ate my food, too." Chakakuka told him that they could no longer share food, and he said that was OK by him. After acknowledging this, they still managed to remain friends.

Chakakuka and Jason visited each other from time to time, but no longer shared food. Whenever it was time for Jason to eat, Chakakuka would leave, and whenever it was time for Chakakuka to eat, Jason would leave and go home.

The next morning there were sounds of gunfire, so we were not allowed to go out to play. We spent all day in the room just lying down and listening to the sounds of gunshots outside. At night we could hear men walking outside talking, unsure if it was government soldiers or the rebels, and sometimes we could hear sounds of people running.

The shooting went on for days, and for days we were kept inside the room with my mother. She cooked in the room, and when she was done, she would feed us quietly so that no one knew we had food. She also made hot water, put it in a bucket, and wiped down our skin. Sometimes when the food was not enough, my mother would feed us and go to bed hungry, just so we would not starve. Because she was constantly hungry so we could eat, she developed an ulcerous stomach.

Our family had a room in the house with no washroom. The adults bathed themselves outside in an outdoor shower spot that was built with zinc and wood with some rocks. My mother would sometimes use the shower spot outside, or would wait until we were asleep and give herself a sponge bath. She kept a medium-sized bucket in the room that we used to pee or poop in, and then in the morning she would take it into the bush and throw the waste away. After, she would wash the bucket with soap and Clorox to make sure there was no contamination so we would not get sick.

It wasn't long until Jamaica Road got a cholera outbreak and people started dying. I know you are probably wondering what cholera is. It is an infectious and often fatal bacterial disease of the small intestine, typically contracted from infected water supplies, and it causes severe vomiting and diarrhea. There were rebels and government soldiers shooting at one another and there was no way for people to go out to get help.

There was this old man named Thomas who lived in one of the rooms all by himself, because his family had left him behind. He was too old to escape the war, and with no one to take care of him, he caught the cholera illness and not long after died. One day, when the shooting had subsided, we were allowed to play with the other kids who lived in some of the rooms in the house. We learned about the old man's death and it made us really scared to even go by his room. Each time that we would get close to his room, we would start running.

My mother waited for the shooting to ease a little, and then she locked us in the room and told us she was going to see our stepfather's friend to get some food, and that she would be back soon. Before our stepfather left for his trip, he told his Lebanese friends who owned a supermarket to give us whatever food we needed until he got back. My mother left to go get some food for us and we waited for what seemed like forever. When she returned, she had a lot of food and she put it all in cardboard boxes so that others were unaware of it, for fear of getting robbed or killed.

My mother brought in all kinds of foodstuffs from the supermarket. There was a certain butter that she brought; I do not remember the name of it, but it was extremely delicious with rice.

My mother would quietly cook some rice with lunchmeat and add her magical delicious butter to it and feed us each with a spoon until the rice was done. I could have eaten it all day, but we had to be careful with how much food we ate so that it lasted until things settled.

The rebels were pretty close, so we were no longer allowed to go out as much. We only went out of the room if my mother was outside. She would ask us to come out for a little bit to play right in front of the house with the other kids who shared it.

One day while we were out playing in front of the house, there was a little girl with swollen feet walking alone with no parents by her side to protect her. Her feet were terribly swollen, her belly was big, and she looked like she hadn't eaten in days.

She went from place to place begging for food, and no one would help her. Every house she went to would shun her and ask her to never come back. I begged my mother to help the girl, to give her some food, but my mother said she wasn't sure what sickness the girl had and she was not going to risk getting us sick. Still, with the heart of a mother, she called the girl and gave her something to eat and drink. The girl could barely eat, but she tried. My mother asked where her parents were, and she said in such a low, sad voice that they got lost and that she could not find them.

My mother asked the girl where she was living, and she said she had nowhere to stay and that she just slept out in the street wherever she could lay her head.

My mother wasn't sure what sickness the little girl suffered from, and due to the fact that she was alone with three kids, she didn't want to add a fourth child, especially a sick one. My mother promised the girl that the only help she was able to give was something for her to eat each time she came around. The girl would come each day and my mother would give her something to eat, and then she would say thanks and leave.

One day the girl stopped coming to visit and it made my mother concerned. She went around asking the neighbours if they had seen her. The neighbours said they too had not seen her in a few days, and they had been wondering what happened because she had been very regular. After a couple more days, my mother went inquiring about the little girl. She later found out that the little girl's legs had gotten extremely bad. They swelled up and burst open, and not long after, she died.

The news of the little girl's death really disturbed my mother and she would stay inside all day and cry. She tried to hide it, but I was that child who always noticed when things were wrong with her. That night, the rebels had gotten really aggressive and the government soldiers were losing ground. All night there were sounds of gunfire and rocket launchers, and my mother put us all flat on the ground to sleep to avoid stray bullets.

She got on her knees and prayed to Jehovah God to guide us and protect our lives. The shooting went on all night until the early morning, and then it subsided for a bit. We did not sleep all night but lay down in fear of our lives. At 5:00 a.m., my mother had us wake up, change our clothes, and put on our shoes, and then she gave us something to eat. By 7:00 the shooting started, and it got worse so everyone in the house had to lock their doors and get out to run to safety.

Almost everyone was out of the house except a selfish old man who did not like kids. He was a friend of the other old man who had died. He was too old and could barely walk, so he decided to stay and accept his fate. We were all standing outside, scared, not sure what to do. My mother did not know which way to go, but she decided that she would run with us to where the crowd of people was heading. She tied Yahgahbo on her back, took Chakakuka in one hand, and me in the other.

There was shooting coming from all directions, and behind us rockets were exploding, and people started running. My mother, with all the confusion, still tried to hold onto Chakakuka and me and run at the same time, but in the process I slipped out of my mother's hand and got lost in the crowd. In the moment I lost my mother, I became frozen out of fear. I just stood there crying and screaming my mother's name as people ran past me to safety.

While standing there all alone and crying, my mother came back for me, took my hand, and said, "Hold on to me and don't let go!" and she held my hand tightly. People were yelling, screaming, shouting, and running for safety. We didn't know where we were going, we just kept running and keeping low so we would not get hit by stray bullets. My mother had heard of a place where the United Nations were giving people free food, but by the time we got there the lineup was huge. We waited for what seemed like all day just to get something to eat.

Then, from nowhere, a lady showed up, willing to help my mother get us to the front of the line for some food. At the front of the line, people were pushing one another desperately to get food for their families as well.

We all made it to the front of the line, including the woman and her family. My mother said thanks to the lady for helping us. We managed to get food, but now we needed a place to stay until things settled. The United Nations had a waiting area for women and children, so we had to wait there until it was safe enough to return.

We waited until the next morning, and my mother got us up and we walked back to Jamaica Road. There were homes that were destroyed by the rockets and a lot of people lost everything except their lives. Along the way, my mother had made friends who gave her information about the area we were staying in and told her that the house in which we lived was untouched by the rebels, there were just a few gunshot hits. When we got to the house, a lot of the people who once lived there with their kids were gone. My mother stayed because she was waiting for our stepfather to come and get us.

There were still a few other people who returned to the house with their families, and that made my mother feel a little safer knowing that we were not staying in the house alone. The government soldiers managed to push the rebels back. I'm not sure where the rebels went, but it was quite far away. As things started to settle a bit, families moved out of the house to find their relatives.

A bit worried but still with a great deal of hope, my mother waited patiently for my stepfather to return from Nigeria. Every week, as another family moved out, my mother wondered if we would be left alone in the house. The old man who could not escape when the rebels attacked had children who had come to get him. I was surprised to see that this old man who didn't like the sounds of kids running around actually had kids of his own.

Not long after the old man left with his family, my stepfather arrived. My mother heard a knock on the door, and at first she thought it must be one of the neighbours in the house, but when she opened the door it was my stepfather, who had come back to get us. She couldn't believe who she was looking at; she screamed for joy and jumped on him with her arms wide open. My stepfather was so happy to see us alive that he started to cry, because he knew that he only left so he wouldn't get killed by the rebels.

My stepfather brought many things for us from Nigeria. He even brought a specially made outfit for my mother and asked her to put it on.

She looked beautiful in it. She wore her outfit all day, and when she took a nap in it, he took her photo on a Polaroid camera and showed it to her after she woke up from her sleep. That photo became one of her favourite photos, because it reminded her of her struggle alone without him and her hope as she waited for his return.

In no time, my stepfather found a place for us to stay on Caldwell Road, but it needed a clean-up first. He said that once the place was all nice and clean, we would move in. My stepfather said it was a big house and that my sister Yahgahbo and I would share a room and my brother Chakakuka would have his own. We were excited and could not wait to see what this place looked like. My stepfather had the whole house painted before we moved in.

He said that the house was big, with a fenced yard large enough for us to go out and play in. He said there were lots of trees in the yard. Coconut trees, banana trees, soursop trees, and flowers. The day came for us to leave. We said our goodbyes to those who were still there and went to see our new home and our new environment.

# Chapter 6

# A STRANGER IN OUR HOUSE

The place on Caldwell Road was very big and had a nice yard, but we had no idea that it was haunted. There was a story about the man who used to own it: he was very jealous and abusive to his wife and one day he killed her in the house.

This house was located beside a river, and it was rumoured that people always found dead bodies by the river. We were excited about moving into such a big house. Even though it had three bedrooms, our parents still had the three of us share one bedroom. When we told my mother that my stepfather had said that Yahgahbo and I would share a room and Chakakuka would have his own, she said, "Your dad is using the other room for his storage place for all his stuff."

We moved lots of stuff into the house that needed unpacking, so it took our parents a few days to settle us in. But they got it done, and the place turned out so nicely, and finally we were home. Our parents decided to get house servants to clean the house and watch over us, so our grandmother Stuciah suggested to my mother that a young man from the village should come live with us, and that it would be OK. My grandmother said that he would be a twenty-four-hour help to us.

Things were talked over with our parents, and the next thing we knew this young man came to live with us. We were asked to call him Uncle Shammi. Our parents said Uncle Shammi would be staying with us to watch over us and make sure everything was OK when they weren't home. Uncle Shammi was about eighteen to twenty years old. He could not speak

English very well when he came to live with us, and when he spoke we found it very funny. Some of the words he would say just made us laugh.

For example, when we were eating dinner and he did not like what was on the table, he would say, “Ma, I am enough,” and that would make us laugh harder. Uncle Shammi was asked to share our bedroom with us, but he slept on the floor while we slept on the bed. Uncle Shammi pretended to be very obedient to our parents and everyone that came around, so our parents started liking him, and promised to send him to a school close to home so he could learn how to speak well and have decent conversations with people.

I’m not sure if I should say that my parents sending him to school was a big mistake, but in many ways it was. Our parents did not know Uncle Shammi was sexually active, so as soon as he knew how to put his sentences together, he started asking the next-door neighbour’s wife to go out with him. At first, the neighbour’s wife thought it was a joke, and that he was just a young boy with a crush on her, but it was no joke. Uncle Shammi told her that he was not a little boy, that he was old enough to have sex and that he had been having sex before coming to live with us.

The neighbour’s wife saw it as a concern, because our parents had two little girls living at home and thought our parents should know about this. She came over and informed our parents what Uncle Shammi had been up to, and even showed them a letter he wrote to her. She told them to keep an eye on him and be careful.

You can imagine how furious this news made our stepfather! He called Uncle Shammi, and in her presence confronted him about what the neighbour’s wife said. Uncle Shammi denied every bit of it. Our parents apologized to the woman and promised it would never happen again. After the woman left, Uncle Shammi got the beating of his life. Our parents threatened to take him out of school; they said there was no point in sending him there when all he does is learn to write letters to people’s wives.

My mother visited our grandmother and told her she would like to return Uncle Shammi, because he was too much for them and was not the young boy he pretended to be. My mother was also mad that our grandmother did not tell her that Uncle Shammi was sexually active. Our grandmother said she did not know such a thing, and that he appeared innocent. Our grandmother told my mother that she had no space left in her house because she had taken more children to live with her and begged for our parents to have more patience with Uncle Shammi, assuring them he would make a change.

Our parents agreed and brought Uncle Shammi back home, hoping for a change. Uncle Shammi forgot how old he was and started playing with us as his equal. One night when our parents were out, Uncle Shammi suggested we all play hide and seek. He told Chakakuka he would be the first to choose his partner, so he chose me while Chakakuka chose Yahgahbo as his. Uncle Shammi first allowed my brother and sister to hide then we went to find them. Next it was our turn, so he suggested we hide in the guest washroom. He said it would be hard for my brother and sister to find us. For me it seemed all fun, but I did not know Uncle Shammi's intentions, and when I found out it was not fun for me anymore, but rather very scary.

When we went in the washroom to hide, Uncle Shammi locked the door. When I asked why, he told me it was so it wouldn't be easy for my brother and sister to come in. The next thing I knew, Uncle Shammi took out his penis and asked me to touch it. I remember telling him, "No, it is too big." He told me touch it, that it would not hurt me, and he tried forcing me to touch it. Just then Chakakuka knocked on the washroom door, and I could hear him tell Yahgahbo that they had searched the whole house and the only place left was the guest washroom.

Chakakuka said, "I know you people are in there, come out!" I was safe for the moment, but not for long because Uncle Shammi had just found his new toy. At night when we went to bed, Uncle Shammi would wait for Chakakuka and Yahgahbo to fall into a deep sleep then he would climb on our bed and try to sleep beside me and touch me while I was sleeping. When I woke up and asked what he was doing, he would say the ground was too hard and sleeping on it was causing him body pain, so he came up on our bed.

In Africa, some parents make it hard for you to talk to them. Our parents were of that kind: we could not easily talk to them because they would beat us for everything, so I could not really tell them what Uncle Shammi was trying to do to me. My brother used to shower with my sister and me because we were very little. We would fill the tub up with water and swim in it, but we were surprised when Uncle Shammi jumped in the tub with us.

He was a big person, so having him in the tub left us without enough space for the rest of us. I remember that we asked him why he had hair on the front of him, but he said nothing about it. Every time we had a bath, Uncle Shammi would jump in and try to touch me.

At one point, I screamed that something had poked me and Uncle Shammi said it was a shark. My brother and sister started yelling along with him, pretending it was a shark, but I knew it wasn't. I knew he was trying to touch me under the water. Our parents did not know all of this was going on and I did not know how to tell them. Our parents hired three female housecleaners to take care of us, and I became very happy. Now I would be safe from Uncle Shammi, because one of the housecleaners was asked to stay with us at home for twenty-four-hour care.

I cannot really remember the name of the older lady who was asked to stay over at the house, but Uncle Shammi did not like her at all because he could not do what he been trying to do to me. She was there to give us baths and make sure we were doing OK, while the other women were there to cook and clean the house and do laundry. We had all these housecleaners working for us because our parents were businesspeople and they were never home to spend time with us.

I am not sure what business our dad did, but we knew what our mother was doing. She sold women things like earrings, bracelets, handbags, wigs, scarfs, cream and lotions, perfumes, sunglasses—you name it. Each time they came back home from their trips, they would bring us nice and expensive stuff. We had everything kids could need, but what we did not have was enough time with our parents because they were always gone, and when they were home it was so much fun.

When both parents were home at the same time, we would sometimes play them against each other. We would ask our mother for something, and when she said no, we would ask our stepfather and he would say yes. Sometimes when our stepdad said no, we would ask our mother and she would say yes.

The new house did not change our stepfather's mind about his intense discipline. I'm not sure what we did this one time, either our parents had a visitor and we were disturbing them or it was something else we did, but the day after, early in the morning, our dad woke us up for punishment. Our parents loved to have big wooden statues in the house, so that was what our stepfather used for punishment that morning.

He told us each to take one statue and pump tire with it, and if we moved from our spots he would whip us very hard. By the time we were done we weren't able to walk. My mother would sometimes tell him that it was too much, but he would not listen, so she would just walk away. We pumped tire that morning along with some good old whippings. When our parents travelled, I always got very sick, while Chakakuka and Yahgahbo behaved as if they were on vacation.

One thing I was known for was that my dreams always came true. My mother got to stay home, and our stepfather travelled for a month, which to me seemed like forever. My mother was in the kitchen cooking one day while I had a nap in our parents' bedroom, and I had a dream. In my dream, our dad was home and we were watching TV. He was watching sports and I wanted to watch cartoons. When I woke from my sleep, I told my mother about the dream. The minute I got through telling her, the doorbell rang, and guess who it was?

My mother said, "Wow, Arnelle just talked about the dream she had of you, that you were home, and here you are." We were so excited to see him. Each time our parents returned from a trip they would also bring for us lots of stuff, including a specific biscuit, which was always a favourite of mine, and is even now. It is called shortbread biscuit, and even today I cannot stop loving it.

Our parents got us registered at an international school called Mounsorado International. The school was known for accepting rich people's kids and it was well run; every government official and businessman and woman had their kids at that school. There was one teacher who made sure every student would never forget his name: Mr. Method-Method.

After coming to Canada and learning what abuse is all about, I would say that this person really abused the students at Mounsorado International School. He would sometimes use a whip or belt on his students, and they got hurt very badly. One day, he made a mistake and whipped me because he said I was late to class after lunchtime. First thing the next morning, my mother was at the school with a very strong warning that if Mr.

Method-Method ever touched any of us again he would lose his job as a teacher, because he would be locked up in jail for physical child abuse.

Every parent complained to the principal about Mr. Method-Method, so he was given a strong warning that the next time there was a complaint about him they would ask him to leave the school. Mr. Method-Method still did not listen; one day he whipped the wrong kid. The boy's name was Shed, he was a teenager whose parents were very rich, and he was very spoiled. Every teenage girl wanted to be with him.

Mr. Method-Method shamed Shed in front of everyone by whipping him badly. The next morning, Shed came to school with a gun and threatened to kill Mr. Method-Method. The entire school was in shock. Shed told Mr. Method-Method to get down on his knees, then took the whip from him and whipped the hell out of him in front of the entire school. That was a moment no student will ever forget.

Shed was asked by the principal to leave the school and never return. She told him she understood how he felt about what Mr. Method-Method did to him and that what he did wasn't right, but bringing a gun to school wasn't the right way to go about it because other kids were going to think it was OK to bring a gun to school to use on other teachers. Mr. Method-Method was called to the office immediately and asked to leave the school for his abuse toward students.

Things at school went well; I made new friends and had new teachers. I got to like it very much, because it was much bigger than my last one and there were more fun things to play with in the playground. We easily adjusted to our school, so our parents had to get a driver for us. Because the driver was always late for work we always got to school late, so my mother decided it was time for her to learn how to drive.

My stepfather kept promising that he would teach my mother how to drive, but he didn't, so my mother got sick of waiting for him to teach her. One day, he went on a business trip and that is when she asked my stepfather's best friend John to teach her how to drive. John said that my mother was so smart that it took her only a day to learn how to drive, but I know someone who wasn't going to be happy to hear the news, and that person was my stepfather.

When he learned that my mother was driving, he got very angry and asked who had taught her how to drive. She told him it was his best friend

John. My stepfather said in an angry voice that his best friend was my mother's lover, and that is why he taught her how to drive. He said it was because John wanted to make himself look like the better person.

My stepfather got very mad and beat my mother up badly. He and his friend had a huge argument and ended their friendship. He told John to never come to our house ever again. The beating of my mother became a habit for Mr. AmiShasi, he was now beating her for almost everything. Even when they went out to eat dinner and a friend she had known for a long time or someone she went to school with said hi to her, there was going to be a fight when they got home, and he would accuse her of dating the person.

He would beat her as he told her that the person who greeted her at dinner was her boyfriend, and even if she said it was not true, he would force her to lie about it and he would beat her repeatedly. He would sometimes give her a book and tell her to make a list of the men she slept with. But because he would not believe her, she had to make up lies and stories about herself, but he would still beat her. One day he brought home a big bundle of whips, and we knew who it was for because he always used his belt on us.

My mother, being attractive, became the envy of every woman around and was admired by every man. Mr. AmiShasi know that my mother had a huge passion for business and decided to give her some money and show her where to travel and bring back stuff to sell. Her great sense of fashion made her the best and most successful woman in town. Everyone knew her for her fine taste in cosmetics, jewels, women's clothing, and wigs. She became a well-known businessperson, and because of her hard work, life was made easy for us.

When it was time for school, our mother would shower us and put our school uniforms on us and make sure our hair was nicely done with the most beautiful hair wrap a girl could wear. We wore the best shoes to school, and all of the teachers knew us, they knew how much our mother loved us and it showed in all she did for us.

All the kids at school wanted to be our friends, they would even line-up to take turns sharing their lunch with us because my mother would put so much food in our lunch kits. I don't remember the name of one particular teacher, but she would always tell one of my friends to eat alone because she was going to eat some of my food. My friend would get mad and tell me that I should make a report to my mother about what the teacher was doing, but I really didn't care much about food so I didn't see it as a problem to make a report about.

# CHAPTER 7

# BUSY BUSINESS-PARENT

One day, our parents had a visitor at our home, so they sent us to watch cartoons in their bedroom. Every second there was a complaint about who got the remote and didn't want to share, or the cartoon that was on was not what the other person wanted to watch. We knew very well not to disturb our parents when they had guests, so they got mad and told Uncle Shammi to turn the TV off. Uncle Shammi came into the room and said, "You guys get out of the room because your parents want me to lock the door." We hesitated, and took our time leaving the room. This made Uncle Shammi mad and he wouldn't wait for us to get out. We left the bedroom, but we still peeked through the space between the door and the wall. I didn't realize my finger was in the door until Uncle Shammi closed it. I gave the loudest scream of my life.

My parents left their guest and came running to their bedroom to find out what had happened. Upon arriving they found my hand covered in blood and discovered that my finger had been sliced open right to the bone. They emptied a bottle of rubbing alcohol into a bowl, because they did not know what else to do and I was bleeding badly. Their friends suggested they take me to the hospital, but my stepfather suggested they take me to his Uncle AmiShasi's clinic for treatment. We got there and my finger was numb by the time we got to meet the doctor, who was the uncle to my stepfather, and they both shared the same name.

My finger got treated and they wrapped a cloth around my neck so that it would hold my hand up for better circulation. My father was so mad he had gone home and beat up Uncle Shammi for not being careful. My hand was healing, but the cloth had gone inside the skin and the skin was healing with the cloth inside.

When we got to the clinic for treatment of my finger, the doctor told my parents to go home and soak my hand in a bowl of rubbing alcohol, and once the skin and the cloth had softened they should slowly pull out the cloth from inside the skin. This was a very painful experience for me, one that I will never forget.

My mother always took good care of us when she was home and not working. She would cook and bake and always want lots of kids over to visit. In the morning when she was giving us a ride to school, she would pick up other kids on the road who also needed a ride. She made friends one day with a kid named Dodobar, he was his parent's only kid, and when he learned my mother had three little kids he was very happy. He told his parents that he met a lady who gave him ride to school every morning. She had three kids who attended the same school as him.

His parents were very glad and asked to meet my mother; she agreed and met his parents. When both parents got to know each other, Dodobar was welcome over to play with us.

Dodobar became our second brother and my mother found her second son. In the morning, my mother would make four lunches for school instead of three. Dodobar became a part of our family and his family and my family attended the same church: the Kingdom Hall of Jehovah's Witnesses. Therefore, when it was time to meet at the Kingdom Hall, we would all dress up and drive together.

Attending meetings at the Kingdom Hall of Jehovah's Witnesses was the best decision my mother ever made; it kept me focused and out of Satan's way. I very much love learning about Jehovah God and how our Earth was made and his purpose for us on it and how much love his son has for us, about how it cost him his life as a sacrifice so that we can all be given a chance to live again on this paradise Earth forever. I was also excited about learning from some of the great men and women of Earth, and what lessons of their lives are important for us to learn from.

One of my favourite lessons was about King Solomon; he was named the wisest man ever to live and walk the surface of the Earth. He became the wisest man by asking Jehovah God not for riches or power, but for wisdom, because he said with wisdom he can rule the world. Jehovah God blessed him with more than that and that is why he is known as the wisest man ever to walk the face of the Earth. As a little girl, every night and each day when I prayed, I asked Jehovah God to please bless me with knowledge, wisdom, understanding, and thinking abilities.

Jehovah God has blessed me with more than I have asked him for and He is still blessing me with more than my requests. I am truly blessed to be favoured by Jehovah God and his son Jesus Christ. My interest in knowing about Jehovah God and his son became so deep that I asked for someone to give me Bible study.

The more I learn about Jehovah God and his interest in us, the more I learn that a lot of things we humans do are so wrong, and it pains Jehovah knowing that we are destroying the most important gift he's given us: the gift of life. Learning from the Bible is the best history of humankind I have ever read. The Bible warns us about everything good and bad, but we as humans want to know what will happen if things aren't done the way we are instructed to do them and, well, we do everything wrong the first time before we realize, and then we start over doing things the right way.

Life at home got a bit more normal until Uncle Shammi decided that he wasn't finished exploring his new toy. My parents travelled and I got sick from missing them. The lady who was asked to give us twenty-four-hour care, Ma Nance, put down some blankets in the living room, laid me on the floor, and covered me with a bedsheet. She took a cold, wet towel and put it on my head so that my fever could break.

When no one was paying attention, Uncle Shammi would pretend to be sleepy, bring a bedsheet, and lay right behind me. He would put his finger between my legs and finger me. I would just lay there and allow him to do it because I was too scared to tell anyone. This went on for a little bit, until Ma Nance started noticing that each time she lay me down, Uncle Shammi would pretend to be sleepy. So one day, Ma Nance asked him, "Why you always lying beside this girl? When she lying sleeping in the room, you are there. When she lying in the living room, you are there. So, you get sleepy every time she is sleeping, right?" Uncle Shammi got mad and said, "So, what are you trying to say?" Ma Nance said, "You need to find somewhere else to sleep, but not beside her." She went on to say that I was sick, and I needed my space.

Uncle Shammi got mad, picked up his blanket, and walked away. Since Uncle Shammi knew Ma Nance was paying close attention to me, he stayed away, but he tried to pick a fight with her. Uncle Shammi said to Ma Nance, "You think I do not know that you were having a thing with the man Deborah left here to help you take care of the kids?" Ma Nance told Uncle Shammi that Jumaryan was a very Christian person and that it was wrong for Uncle Shammi to try and lie on his name. Ma Nance said to Uncle Shammi, "I don't know what is eating you up, but if you bring your nonsense to me, I will not hesitate to jump you for a fight."

Uncle Shammi challenged Ma Nance to a fight, but Jumaryan stepped in and said that he was not going to allow Uncle Shammi to be disrespectful to her. And that if Uncle Shammi cannot show respect to her, he would ask him to leave until our parents returned. Uncle Shammi said to Jumaryan, "This is not your house and you got no right to kick me out, plus I was here before you arrived." He said to Uncle Shammi, "I do not care who was here first, if you do not behave yourself, I will ask you to leave and return when these kids' parents are back from their trip."

I burned with a high fever and grew so sick that I had to get rushed to the hospital. The doctor told Ma Nance and Jumaryan that I was only sick because I missed my parents, but I should be well soon. Jumaryan was a brother at the Kingdom Hall of Jehovah's Witnesses, and so our parents trusted him to stay at home with us. When we got home that day, my mother arrived from her trip alone. I was so happy but too sick to even stand to greet her, so they lay me back down and I was given special attention.

When my mother was home, she would cook and invite all the children in the neighbourhood to come and eat with us. It did not matter if they were rich or poor, she would put everything in the same bowl for us to eat together. After, we would play outside together. I liked to climb the coconut tree and swing on its branches, until one day when I fell into the thorn bushes and got poked everywhere.

They say when you are a child you have lots of dreams, but not all dreams come true. Some would and some would not, but you have to keep trying and believing in yourself and most of your dreams will come true. I have been known to dream a lot and my dreams always came true. Life wasn't all that better between my mother and my stepfather, but my mother tried to keep a steady home for us to stay in so she took a lot from Mr. AmiShasi, like the beating and control.

Our grandmother Stuciah wasn't happy that life was getting a bit better for my mother, so she started coming over all the time to beg my mother for money. When my mother gave it to her, she would spend it on God knows what or who and then she would come back for more. Therefore, my mother decided not to give her any more money, but she would still come over or send people she lived with to harass my mother for money.

My mother still refused to give her any money, so her mother Stuciah would get aggressive and repeatedly knock on the gate of our yard. When my mother refused to answer, Stuciah started to call my mother all kinds of names, saying that my mother had children by different men and that she would make sure that our father did not marry her.

Our grandmother went to the extent of telling our father that my mother slept around a lot with other men and was not to be trusted, and that awoke his jealousy and insecurity. He stopped trusting my mother with everything she did and everywhere she went. When my mother went out and spent time with her friends, there would be a fight when she returned. He would accuse her of cheating, and we would be in our room crying and wishing we were old enough to help her. We hoped and prayed she would leave him for beating her up, but she was too scared to because being a single mother to three children in Africa was not easy.

She wanted us to have a good life, so she suffered all of his abuse, both physical and emotional. When he took her out to dinner and a male friend said hi to my mother, there was always a big fight when they returned home. He would ask her all these questions and make her lie and admit that she dated these guys, because he said that was the only way he would forgive her, even though it was for something she never did. After admitting to all of it he would still beat her up.

When we would see her in the morning, she would lie to us and say something beat her up in her sleep, and we believed it most of the time, but we were smart enough to know what was going on with the two of them. One day, she told us that he had brought home a gun and said that one day he would use it on her. I'm not sure what I went searching for in my parents' room, but I saw the gun there. At first, I didn't know what it was so I picked it up, but it was too heavy for me. Still curious to know what it was, I took it to my mother who was cooking in the kitchen and asked her what it was.

When she saw the gun in my little hands, she panicked and warned our stepfather to keep his gun out of our reach, because it is very dangerous for kids to be in contact with it. What we also did not know was that our stepfather was buying many guns to take back to Nigeria and many expensive cars and all kinds of stuff. Mr. AmiShasi was a well-known man with lots of connections in the Liberian government.

We didn't know that he and my mother were planning to take us all out of Liberia, because his friends in the Liberian government told him there was going to be more war coming very soon and that we should leave the country and travel elsewhere for safety. So, one night while we were all asleep, the Liberian minister of foreign affairs came over to our house with our passports, and because we were too little and too sleepy to sign it, the minister just used our fingerprints for our signature.

We had our visas and everything to travel to Switzerland to stay and go to school until things were back to normal in Liberia. We did not know all that was going on, because we were much too young to understand.

My mother and stepfather left on their last business trip together. Apparently, my mother was to come back and collect all her money from those who owed her and then we were to leave the country, but my mother was a very foolish woman and loved the people who never gave a damn about her, but who only envied her from day one.

She told her sister Wawanibo that she was leaving the country for a little while with her kids, and that she would be back, but Wawanibo begged my mother to stay just a little while longer. She said that if she left, she would really miss her.

My mother always had a passion for her sister Wawanibo, so she agreed to stay a while longer, even though she was told not to stay for more than a few days in Liberia. She was instructed by our stepfather to get us and leave, but her agreeing to stay a while longer changed our destiny for life. A week after she decided to stay, I had a dream that there was a war going on and there was shooting everywhere, and when I woke up and told my mother about my dream, she told me the rebels were far away and they wouldn't be able to come around anytime soon.

What we didn't know was that the rebels had been in the city for a while, behaving like village people who came to visit family members, and they were awaiting the order to carry on. The morning after my dream, we woke up to lots of noise everywhere and people running and yelling and crying. My mother told us not to go outside. She went to ask the neighbour what was happening and was told that the area had been captured by the rebels and they were not allowing anyone to enter or leave the area.

That was when my mother realized that Mr. AmiShasi was right about everything and that she had made a big mistake by listening to Wawanibo. She told us to pack up few things and head over to see a lady named Morlin, who attended the same Kingdom Hall of Jehovah's Witnesses as we did. We were not sure what to do, but we packed whatever we could and headed over to Morlin's house to stay for a bit, and we wished that things would get better so we could travel.

Morlin had two sons and a daughter, and her husband was in the United States of America. He took care of them from there. When we arrived at Morlin's house, things with the war got more heated so there was no way my mother could go and get whatever things Mr. AmiShasi asked her to get out of the house.

My mother waited for a week until things calmed a bit, then she took some area boys with her to check on our home. When she got there, she found that almost all our things were looted but she managed to bring food that we could use to survive on until God only knows when. My mother was very sad, because she knew losing Mr. AmiShasi's things to the rebels wasn't going to make him a happy man when he heard about it. But Morlin encouraged my mother by saying that Mr. AmiShasi would understand and would be glad that we were alive.

All Mr. AmiShasi's guns and expensive cars were gone, so I wasn't sure if that news was going to make him a happy man, but you will learn about this later on in this book. The most important things that my mother kept on her were our passports and the ten thousand dollars he gave us to use for travel. During the nights at Morlin's house, there was lots of gunfire; they call it the "sound of music" because it really did sound like music to the ears, but very scary, too. But the more you heard it, the more you got used to the sound of it. At night, no one was allowed to make a sound or even have any lights on inside the house, so when my mother wanted to cook at night she would use a flashlight just to see what she was cooking. When it was time to eat, we were not allowed to use spoons for fear that they would make noise and the rebels would be aware that people were living in the house.

We would all wash our hands very quietly and eat without making a single sound. At night when it was time to sleep, my mother was afraid of one of us getting hit by a stray bullet, so we would all lay on the floor, including Morlin and her kids, and we would put the mattress on top of us. If there was a stray bullet, it would only bounce off the bed and we would all be protected.

But no matter what happened, we always did a group family study together and we all asked Jehovah God to guard us through those difficult times, and Jehovah God kept his promise to us and truly did protect us. One morning my mother went out to ask the neighbour for water for us to all drink, and while she stood and waited, a stray bullet passed right by her ear. Another time everyone went outside for some fresh air to chat, because the shooting had stopped for a little while. We all decided to go back inside from sitting under the coconut tree, and a rocket exploded and split the coconut tree in half as soon as we had entered the house and locked the door.

The spot the rocket exploded on was the very spot my mother was sitting. That was one example of the way Jehovah God protected his people, showing us that we were truly protected by Him and his son and angels. Now there was more fear of ever leaving the house, so we were told that we were no longer allowed to go outside, even for fresh air, because it was no longer safe. Although things were bad and we were all stuck, we kept ourselves entertained by making jokes or talking about other people's most funny life experiences during the day, and at night we would pray and lay back under the mattress for safety.

We did that for about a month, and just when we thought things were going to go back to normal, the rebels came with reinforcements and took over the other rebels. These ones were all friendly, even though none of them seemed nice. Intense shooting went on for days, and the people of the area started to slowly disappear. We weren't sure what was happening to them, but we were still sure the neighbours that lived closer to Morlin's house were OK.

Once in a while, during the day, we would still hear them talk. We started to run out of food, so my mother warned us not to waste any of it, and told us that whatever we could not finish we should save for later, because we would need it. In the midst of the war, we found a way to keep ourselves happy.

While lying under the mattress, we would tell stories to one another and sometimes we would laugh, but not loud enough for someone outside to hear us. Sometimes Morlin or my mother would come into the room to tell us to keep our noise down, because we were getting loud and they did not want the rebels knowing there were people in the house. When Morlin and my mother were done cooking, we would all sit in the hallway to quietly eat our food.

We usually sat with our backs touching the columns of the hall, so we never sat close to one another, but we also did not sit too far away, either. But the minute we heard shooting close to the house, we would all get very close together and start praying for our lives. My mother tried to hold Chakakuka, Yahgahbo, and me in her arms to reassure us that we were safe.

When the shooting got heavy, we would all crawl into the bedroom and lay under the mattress. But with everyone under the mattress, the room started to get really hot, and underneath that mattress we could barely get air to breathe. We would say, "Mama, we can't breathe," and our mother would say, "OK, just poke your head out a little bit for fresh air, but no lifting your head, because I do not want any of you to get hit by stray bullets." When we poked our head out, it felt good having the relief of being able to breathe again and not suffocate.

# CHAPTER 8

# THE DISTANCE WE WOULD NEVER FORGET

We woke up to a huge pounding on the door very early in the morning. At that time of the morning, we knew it was not the neighbour who was pounding on the door. We knew it was the rebels. He knocked and knocked, and we were all too afraid to make a sound, so we heard him say he would count from one to five and if no one answered, when he entered the house he would kill everyone in it. When he started at one, my mother yelled, "We are here, please don't shoot us!"

He then asked who all was inside and my mother said just women and kids. The rebels told us to come out quickly and not to carry anything with us, because the other rebels ahead were not nice. He said that if our mothers had money or any documents, they should get rid of them, because if the other rebels see them on us they would kill us all. Therefore, the passports my mother had for us to travel with and the $10,000 cash money were thrown into the bush, to where we cannot remember.

We started on our journey. I didn't have any footwear because we were in such a rush to leave the house. As we walked, there were lots of people walking in front of us, some with bundles on their heads, some with babies on their backs, and some with their elderly parents in a wheelbarrow. There were kids who got separated from their parents in the crowd; there were people wearing just their nightwear because they had no time to put clothes on.

As we walked many miles, we came to a place with dead bodies lying on the ground. There were so many of them piled up together they made a hill. I asked my mother who they were; I remember her saying they were dead bodies, and we just kept walking. We walked a little more and there were dead soldiers lying all around the place, and at that moment we became fearless because we had to survive. Any indication of fear would call the rebel's attention, and then the very thing that scared us would be the thing we would become a part of, just like those who were dead.

The army jet planes were called jet bombers, because they would just fly over and drop bombs without calculating if there were rebels or innocent people, including children. When we heard it coming, we all lay flat in the mud so they wouldn't see us, while others would run to a big tree in the forest that had lots of shade. We walked for hours and got really hungry, but there was a cassava farm just a short distance away, so everyone ran to it to get some cassava to eat. We heard voices from inside the small house on the farm telling us to leave their cassava alone. The crowd of people responded by telling them to come outside and stop them.

We were over five hundred people; how could they have stopped us? They were so afraid, they did not say another word. Everyone got enough to eat, but there was no water to drink. From others in the crowd, we learned that there was a river, but it was far from where we were, so we all tried our best to walk a bit faster to get to where the water was before it started getting too late. When we got to the river, there was no thought to whether the water was clean or not, everyone just jumped in and started drinking it. The next thing we saw were dead bodies floating down the river stream.

When my mother saw that there were dead bodies in the river, she immediately felt sick and her throat started to hurt. It kept getting worse over the hours of travel. We came to a checkpoint and the rebels separated the males from the females, while the women waited for the men to be checked. The rebels made an announcement that they would be checking every man for any marks on their skin. They said that if they found any, they would need an explanation, because members of other rebel groups carried certain marks on them.

The rebels said if the men had no good explanation, they would be accused of being a part of the other rebel groups and they would be killed. My mother was very worried, because Chakakuka did have some marks on him from playing wild and getting himself hurt, and she wasn't sure what the rebels would say about that, but she advised Chakakuka to be brave and tell them the truth about his marks—that he got them from getting hurt while playing.

My mother's friend Morlin's older son Zakneh had marks on his head from being ill. When the rebels called him to ask him why he had so many marks on his head, he was scared and responded by saying that his mother beat him up on his head and that is why he got the marks. The rebels demanded that his mother come forward. They said that if what he was saying was true, that his mother beat him up like that, then she is a very wicked woman and deserves to die. Morlin came forward crying and said that she didn't beat her son up, that he suffered from an illness that left marks on his head.

The rebels got mad and asked why he would lie about his mom like that, but she begged them, saying that her son was scared and did not know what to say, so the rebels let them go.

Walking ahead, we came to another checkpoint where the rebels were checking women and girls only, and if the rebels found you good-looking, they would take you as their wife. While waiting for our turn to get checked, my mother put my sister on her back, because the rebels didn't want a woman with kids because it is too much work to maintain them. Then my mother heard a voice in the crowd; it was our neighbour's daughter calling her. When she recognized who it was, my mother started to ask her about everyone that had stayed over at the neighbour's house, and she told her that her father refused to leave.

She also said that the rest of her family got separated and she didn't know where they were. She then begged my mother to put me on her back to pretend that I was her daughter, so the rebels would not take her away as a wife. My mother agreed and the girl put me on her back.

My mother was ahead of us with my sister on her back. When she got to the checkpoint, the rebels accused my mother of having a baby by a city man while they were alone with no women. They beat my mother while my sister was on her back.

When I saw that, I knew it was my turn to get beaten, because I was on the back of the girl and the rebels didn't ask you to put the child down, they beat you while the child was on your back. So, we got to the rebels, and when they saw the girl they asked her if I was her daughter. She answered yes and the rebels said, "What's a beautiful young girl like you doing having a child?" She had nothing to say, and the rebels were so mad at how beautiful she was they beat us both because they could not take her.

The rebels needed young girls to cook for them, wash their clothes, clean their homes, and have sex with them. We continued walking and met a pregnant woman with just her nightgown on. It was not very long before a stray bullet penetrated her and her nightgown, and she started bleeding. We came to a stop, and the rebels began to check the lineup for anyone they thought suspicious, and when they arrived at the pregnant woman who was bleeding, they decided to bet if she had a boy or a girl in her belly.

One rebel said she was having a boy, and another said she was having a girl, then another rebel said, "How about we find out what it is she's having," and they all agreed and took a knife and opened the woman's belly while she was still alive and took her baby out. It was a baby boy. The other rebel said, "You see, I told you it was a boy," and they left the woman and her baby to die.

We continued with our walk, but the rebels kept taking people out of the line, saying that they worked for the other rebel groups, and all you heard when they took the people into the bush was the sound of gunfire.

A large lady was standing in front of me and apparently she was recognized by one of the rebels as being married to a Mandingo man, so the rebels said to her, "Hey you, I remember you, your husband is Mandingo," and the lady said, "Yes my husband is, but what's wrong with that?" The rebel told her they did not like Mandingo because they killed some of their people, and so they were going to kill her, too. The woman started crying and begging for her life as the rebels took her into the bush. There were sounds of gunfire and I never saw the woman again. To my surprise, I heard a rebel lady speak to my mother, saying, "Hey you, get out of the line and come with me."

Because of what I had seen them do to other people when they took them out of the line, I started crying, but then I said to myself, don't cry, nothing is going to happen to her, just pray to Jehovah God to guide and protect her. Right there and then I prayed to Jehovah God that if He let my mother survive the war I would give my life to Him and be His servant all the days of my life. My mother said at that moment she felt death and she knew that the woman was going to kill her, but she was not ready to give up without a fight.

She said she would rather go down fighting, but within a moment she started to pray to Jehovah God for his protection. As my mother and the woman walked deep into the bush, the woman said to my mother, "Give me six feet," and then the woman put her gun in shoot mode. Right before she could shoot, a voice from behind both of them spoke. It was a man's voice, one of the rebel members. The rebel guy said to the rebel lady, "You will not shoot this lady," and the rebel lady said, "Why are you messing up my shit?"

The guy kept saying to her, "You will not shoot this lady, because if you do I will shoot you and your whole family." My mother said she thought she was dreaming because two rebels were fighting over her; one would have liked to kill her and the other was trying to save her. After more than ten minutes of both rebels arguing, the rebel woman said to my mother, "You are so damn lucky, so you had better thank your God, because if it were not for this asshole fucking my shit up I would have had fun killing you."

After the rebel lady left, the rebel guy told my mother that he remembered her, and right there and then my mother said to herself, *I hope I am not in trouble again; I just hope it is something good.*

The guy then said to my mother, "It was a while ago and I was taking my daughter to school, but the rain was so heavy we couldn't get a taxi. You slowed your BMW down beside us and said that you would be right back after dropping your kids off, and you would give my daughter and me a ride to her school. And I didn't believe you, but you did. You came back and gave my daughter and me a ride to her school and after that you dropped me off at my home, and I couldn't stop thanking you for what you did for us, and since that day I never forgot you."

My mother said she just dropped and started crying. She could not believe the good thing that she did so long ago was what just saved her life. Not long after, I saw my mother coming and I knew then and there that Jehovah God kept his promise to me and saved my mother's life, just as I had asked him to. Although most don't believe that God is real, it is when you find yourself in certain life situations that you see the wonderful works of Jehovah God. My mother gave us all a hug and kept crying and giving thanks to Jehovah God for saving her life, and told us how at first she never thought she would see us again, but she knows having great faith in Jehovah God is very important.

We had to keep moving because it was starting to get late. While walking, the rebel guy that saved my mother's life came running after us, saying that he was going to walk with us all the way to the other rebel's location and then he would leave so we wouldn't get stopped by his rebel group. We walked and walked until we came to a stop at another rebel location. He told my mother that he could not go any further, but he wished us well, and a safe trip to wherever we were going. My mother thanked him for saving her life and ours, and he told us to keep safe and left.

Now we were all alone with some other group of people that were walking in the same direction as us. There was a checkpoint called God Bless You Gate, which meant if you live past that checkpoint God had really blessed you, because not many people walked through it alive. There were dead bodies everywhere, but Jehovah God showed his miracle, because just before our arrival the rebel who was killing people at the checkpoint was told to go see his big boss.

When we arrived, the checkpoint was empty and no one was there, so we all quickly walked through it and escaped being killed. Not long after we left, we learned that when the rebel returned to the checkpoint, he killed everyone that was left behind because he was mad so many people escaped getting killed by him. There was another checkpoint where they were taking all the women and raping them, so when the rebels called my mother, she became very scared and started to pray.

She said four men took her into a room and were about to rape her, but just at that time an army jet plane started flying overhead and the rebels left her and ran to take cover. She said she started to run, and just when she thought she was safe she ran right into a rebel ambush. Another lady was running for her life as well; she held my mother's hand and told her not to run that way because the rebels were there and she would get killed. After my mother left the area and found us, we learned that the rest of the women that were left were raped and killed. It was almost dark and we were still walking, and we came to a location where we met a rebel who said he liked my brother. That made my mother scared, because the rebels took little boys for child soldiers.

The rebel guy asked whose son he was, and my mother came forward. The rebel was a nice guy; he told my mother that he would make sure he got us a ride to Karkata, because it was getting too late and it was not safe for women and children to be walking late at night. He said that anything could happen. He told us to keep walking and that he would meet us ahead. While we were walking, news came from ahead of us that some rebels took a ten-year-old girl to rape her but her grandmother begged the rebels to rape her instead of her grandchild.

The rebels refused and raped the ten-year-old girl and almost killed her while her grandmother watched and cried bitterly. When their big boss heard what they did to the ten-year-old girl, he sent for the three rebels and killed them, and took the old woman and her granddaughter to a nearby clinic. Jehovah God saved us from getting raped first, and we were still very little so there was not much attention on us.

The rebel kept his promise to us and brought a big truck to drive us to Karkata. Being that there were other people who needed a ride for their family, it was a struggle for my family to get on the truck and I almost got left behind. My mother made sure that her friend Morlin and her kids got on the truck, too, and oh, how happy we all were to feel safe again. The truck took us all to Karkata, but by the time we arrived there was no place to stay, so we all went to a big warehouse where all the people who were displaced stayed.

From fear I did not realize that my feet were covered in blisters from walking without any footwear on the hot sand and road. Although my feet started to hurt, I was glad that we were all alive. While trying to sleep at the warehouse, one of the rebel soldiers tried to rape my mother while she was lying beside us.

My mother screamed and everyone woke up, and that is how the guy left her alone. Another rebel soldier came and said he had a place for us to stay. At this point we could not trust anyone, but we went along with him anyway. My mother took her friend Morlin and her kids along with us, and we arrived at a mud hut with not much space in it, but there was about three rooms inside so the guy gave us one room to stay in. Before we could settle, there was a knock on the door.

It was the rebel soldier; he wanted to have a word with my mother, so she went out to talk to him. He told her that he was interested in making her his girlfriend and that she should come and spend the night in his room. She told him that she would be right back, she just needed to put us to bed and then she would come and spend the night with him. When she returned, Morlin asked what the rebel said. When my mother told her, Morlin said my mother shouldn't worry, and that when he came back to knock on the door my mother shouldn't answer. We put stuff behind the door so that he couldn't come in if he tried to break down the door.

We also blew out the candlelight so he would not think that anyone was up. It wasn't long after that this rebel guy came knocking on the door, but no one answered him. He kept knocking and knocking and knocking until he got tired and walked away. The next morning, he was very mad at my mother. He didn't say a word to her, but instead he sent one of the other ladies to tell us that we couldn't stay there, that we had to leave. But the ladies that lived in the mud hut were nice. They said that we could not leave without eating anything, and since they were cooking, we should wait because we had not had anything good to eat.

What the women were cooking was a traditional meal called pepper turburgee. This traditional soup is made with a lot of pepper and meat and other good stuff, and is eaten with rice, but the soup is so spicy that one has to be a real man to eat it. When the women where done cooking, we could barely eat the food because the pepper was too much, even grown men who ate the food were crying. It was time for us to leave and go find a place to stay; we told the women thanks, and off we went.

My mother had studied with Jehovah's Witnesses for many years, so she and Morlin suggested we find the Kingdom Hall of Jehovah's Witnesses and stay there, that way we would be kept safe. My mother asked everyone who walked the road where she could find the Kingdom Hall of Jehovah's Witnesses, and people kept directing us until we found it. When we got there, the brothers and sisters were very happy to see that we all made it alive.

Every family slept on the floor in the Kingdom Hall because there was nowhere to sleep and not much space, but we were all happy to be safe and away from rebel attacks. At night, there would be sounds of gunfire, and sometimes we would hear the rebels walk past the Kingdom Hall and they would say, "These are Jehovah's Witnesses, let's leave them alone." During the morning and day, there would be sisters assigned to make breakfast for everyone, and there were sisters who were assigned to make lunch and dinner for everyone, but my mother was a true mother, she was never OK with the way things were. She was always out there trying to find a way and was always asking questions about how she could get us out of Karkata.

She would go out in the morning, and if she heard news about free food being given to women and kids, she would come to the Kingdom Hall and let all the sisters know to go and get food for their families as well.

I will tell you a brief history about Charles Taylor, the man who became a rebel leader in Liberia and later on became its president. Charles Taylor is a Liberian war criminal and a former politician who later became the twenty-second president of Liberia on August 2, 1997, until his resignation on August 11, 2003. Charles Taylor earned his degree at Bentley, a college in America, after which he came to work in the Liberian government of President Samuel K. Doe. Charles Taylor was later removed from working with the Liberian government due to embezzlement.

He later went to Libya where he was trained as a guerrilla fighter. Upon his return to Liberia, Charles Taylor became head of a rebel group called the NPFL, which stands for National Patriotic Front of Liberia, with the intent of overthrowing the Samuel K. Doe government, which initiated the first civil war of Liberia in 1989. The war lasted from 1989 until 1996, and during that time President Samuel K. Doe was executed, and with that Charles Taylor gained control over a large portion of the country and became one of the most prominent warlords in Africa.

My mother said that one day she went out to look for food for us to eat, and while on her way back, she ran into Charles Taylor and his rebel boys having a meeting, so she stopped to listen to what they were saying. Charles Taylor caught sight of her, but she left quickly so she did not get into more trouble. The next day he had his rebel boys looking for her with a description, so the sisters suggested she stay indoors to be protected.

The rebels came around to ask for my mother, but no one responded and they left. There was a brother from the Kingdom Hall in Karkata named Tumba who knew people who were transporting people to Ivory

Coast, so my mother begged him to help transport us there. He said he would make some arrangements. My mother now had to spend most of her time indoors or disguise herself when she went out, so that the rebels would not find her, because she knew what living with the rebel leader Charles Taylor would mean for her and her children.

It was not long before Tumba told my mother that he had found a transport that would take us to Ivory Coast. Tumba helped my mother get all the necessary papers we would be needing to enter. Morlin decided to stay in Karkata with her children, so my mother got us ready. We said goodbye to the brothers and sisters at the Kingdom Hall and off to Ivory Coast we went. The drive was long. We were told that the driver would be the one doing the translations with the Ivorian Immigration, because we were unable to speak French.

When we arrived in Ivory Coast, the city looked so beautiful, all lit up and so alive. The food there was different and tasted really good. It was very late when we got there so my mother got us a motel to sleep in, and by morning she decided to look for the Kingdom Hall of Jehovah's Witnesses nearby so we could meet with some brothers and sisters.

We took a taxi to the Kingdom Hall, and my mother asked a few questions with a translator and they directed us to a brother from the Kingdom Hall that lived nearby. His name was Philipy. Philipy was a single dad to three boys and had a niece-in-law that he was taking care of living with him. Her name was Valatina. Philipy's wife lived in the USA and Valatina's mother lived in Germany, she was the sister of Philipy's wife, so Valatina's mother was Philipy's sister-in-law.

My mother said she would be leaving us with Philipy for a little bit to go meet with our stepfather in Nigeria, then she would come back and get us. We had never been left to live with anyone before, so being left with Philipy was another major change for us, but, oh well, we had to help our mother make life easier by understanding her and being supportive.

It hurt to be left there, but having other kids around made it easy and distracting. The two younger kids amongst the kids Philipy was taking care of were his little son Ermen and his sister-in-law's daughter Valatina; they were friendly, so it made staying there feel like home. Every morning we had to wake up very early, around 5:30, to brush our teeth and wash our faces because Philipy went jogging.

If we didn't wake up on time, we would get no money to go and buy our breakfast, and he wouldn't return until late afternoon, so that meant you would stay hungry all morning and all afternoon and no one was allowed to give some of their food to you. In the evening, Philipy liked to sit outside the fence of the yard and play his guitar while he sang, but he usually liked to do it late at night. During our bedtime was when Philipy played his guitar, and we were not allowed outside the fence. If anyone wanted to go outside to listen to the songs, Philipy had his own restrictions, which included giving you a whipping on your hand or on your butt with a big wooden stick.

Whoever was able enough to withstand the pain from the whipping was allowed outside the fence late at night to listen to Philipy sing. We all tried, including his son Ermen as well, but not everyone would be allowed outside the fence because not everyone was able to stand the pain. Every morning we would all wake up at 5:30, brush our teeth, and get our breakfast money. As for me, I loved the Ivorian food; their sour milk and something that looks like a donut was always so good. I would buy that all the time, and then for lunch I would buy Ayeekee to eat.

We were not old enough to shower ourselves, but Philipy was like a solider, and with him, you had to learn a lot. He taught us how to shower our skin, because at first we would just put soap and water on our stomach. Philipy had to tell us to wash under our arms, legs, back, face, belly, and feet. He had no one to help fix our hair so he fixed our hair himself—three girls' hair for church and for everyday wear. Philipy was like a father to us; we learned a lot by just staying at his place for some time. In the fenced yard, we were all given a little piece of land to plant something on.

With mine I planted beans, okra, pepper, corn, eggplant, and watermelon. It was the most beautiful thing watching my plants grow each day from seeds to plants, then watching them produce fruits and vegetables. In the morning after brushing our teeth and collecting our breakfast money, we would water our plants before the sun came out. We learned what was good for our plants and what was not good for them, and Philipy would give us advice on how to take care of them because he saw we were all committed to it.

When it was harvest time, it was all the more fun because we now got to eat food from what was once seeds, and all of our hard work and commitment really paid off. One day we all woke up late and Philipy had already gone jogging, so we did not get money for breakfast. Philipy returned from his jogging and we were all complaining how hungry we were. Philipy told us to wait until the big boys in the house were done cooking lunch, and by that time it was after 1 or 2 p.m.

We complained and complained until Philipy got mad and said, "OK, since you guys won't wait till lunch is served, I am going to give you all money to go to the restaurant and buy each of you a very large bowl of rice, and you all better make sure you eat it, because if you don't I will beat you guys up badly for being disobedient." Valatina was asked to eat the big pot of rice with palm butter soup, and we all got a very large bowl of rice from the restaurant.

We started eating but soon we realized we were getting full. Valatina was the first to give up, so she was beaten badly. My sister Yahgahbo was the next person to give up; she was also beaten badly. Chakakuka gave up also and he too was beaten badly, and then Philipy's son Ermen gave up and he was beaten badly.

When it was my turn, I refused to let him beat me up, so I took my own time and ate all my rice. Although I was not beaten up, the pain from over-feeding myself was too much. I held my belly and started crying, and after that day, we made sure to be up on time for our breakfast money. Just when we started getting used to being around Philipy and his children, there was a problem: his wife in America was not happy with the fact that he was helping to take care of us.

She started to complain and said it was getting too expensive for her, and that Philipy should find a way to return us. They would argue about it all the time when she phoned him, and I could tell how hurt he felt because we had no one and nowhere to go, and we were too little for him to leave us just anywhere. But at the same time, he did not want a problem in his family because of us.

So, he contacted my mother and explained the situation to her, that he would be unable to continue taking care of us. She made a few calls and found out that she had a relative named Aunty Umo who lived not too far away, and asked Philipy to take us there. Philipy explained to us that he and his children would be leaving for America and there would be no one to take care of us when he was gone, and that is why he phoned our mother and she told him to take us to her Aunty Umo.

Philipy took us to Aunty Umo's house; it was in a very expensive neighbourhood with swimming pools everywhere, and Caucasian people living there as well. We got to Aunty Umo's house and Philipy rang the bell at the gate. A person came, and Philipy told him we were there to see Aunty Umo, but the person told Philipy that Aunty Umo instructed him to not let anyone in. Philipy demanded that the person give Aunty Umo a call to let her know that we were there to see her; he did, and Aunty Umo still instructed him to make us wait outside her gate.

We waited and waited out in the hot sun, and when Aunty Umo finally arrived she didn't even let us in her house. She made us sit outside on her balcony as she discussed with Philipy what to do with us. She said her home didn't have enough space for us to stay, as she lived with her husband and kids and another relative. Aunty Umo told Philipy to take us to the Liberian refugee camp in Ivory Coast. Philipy told her that we did not enter Ivory Coast as refugees and for that reason we would not be accepted at the camp, especially without our mother. Aunty Umo still insisted they take us to the refugee camp, and that she would talk to someone there to take us.

Aunty Umo entered her car along with Philipy and us, and off to the Liberian refugee camp we went. When we got there, the people refused us saying that we did not enter Ivory Coast as refugees, and they wouldn't allow us to stay there because we had her as a relative and that we were much too small to be left alone. Aunty Umo was very mad and insisted that Philipy take us back to where he came from, because she had her own family to take care of.

She dropped us off outside somewhere and said she had a meeting at the bank. After she left, Philipy explained to us how much he cared for us, that his wife was sending for him and his kids soon, and that when he left there would be no one to take care of us, so he wanted to make sure we were somewhere safe until our mother could come for us or send for us. He told us that he would take us in the taxi back to Aunty Umo's place and leave us at the gate, and when she asked we should tell her that he left us there. And when she asked where he lived, we should say that we don't know the address.

We did just that, according to plan, because Philipy had been very nice to us and we understood his situation and wanted to help him out. Philipy took us in the taxi to Aunty Umo's place and left us there, and told us to ring the doorbell, which we did. The same guy came to the gate and told us that Aunty Umo wasn't home and that we should come back later, but we told him we had nowhere to go and that Philipy left us there and we didn't know where he was staying. So the guy asked one of the older ladies if he should allow us in, and the lady said yes, and they let us in.

They made us wait outside on the balcony for hours before Aunty Umo returned, but before that her kids returned from school and came outside to play with us. When Aunty Umo got home and saw this, she did not like it at all. She was mad at those who let us in and wanted us to leave, but just as Philipy told us, we told her he left us there and we didn't know where he stayed, and she grew angrier knowing that she was stuck with us.

She was still adamant that she wanted to take us to the refugee camp, but her husband, who was a manager at a bank, said no, that they had enough money to take care of us. He even talked about putting us in school since we were going to stay with them, but she strongly disagreed and said that we were not their responsibility, and that she going to make sure she got in contact with our mother to come get her children from her house. Her children and husband were nice to us, but Aunty Umo was not.

When food was served, Aunty Umo's kids were excited for us to eat along with them on the table, but Aunty Umo got mad and said she wouldn't allow us to, because we were not the kind of kids who should eat at her table. She told us to go outside her house and put our food on the ground to eat, so we took our food that they had put in a big bowl for us to eat together and went outside. The ground was our table. When it was night-time, her daughters wanted us to share their bed and they even loaned us their nightgowns, but when Aunty Umo came looking for us, she got really mad when she saw that her daughters had given us their nightgowns to wear.

She screamed and told us to take her daughters' nightgowns off our dirty skin and that her kids would never share anything with us, because we were not the type of children to share things with her kids.

Ashamed, we quickly took her daughters' nightgowns off and put our own clothes back on. When her kids asked her why she would behave like that, she screamed at them and told them to go to bed without a single word from them. We left her kids' bedroom and she took us to a room where we slept on the floor, and she said from then on that was where we would stay. I just could not believe what was happening to us, from living such a good rich life to living homeless and being treated badly.

Every morning before we ate breakfast, Aunty Umo had us kill flies outside before she would give us food. In the evening, it was the same thing, and there were so many flies in Ivory Coast it would take us hours before we could get something to eat. Her husband was a very busy man, so he was unaware of how we were being treated in the house. She made sure that we never got to meet him, because she did not want him to know that we were being treated badly. Each time we would eat outside on the ground, Aunty Umo would come and tell us that our useless mother was busy in Nigeria having fun, and that she did not give a damn about us.

She would comment on how stuck she felt with us, and how she couldn't wait for the day our mother would come to get us. What she did not tell us was that our mother was sending money to take care of us while we stayed at her house. Aunty Umo was just the type who didn't like any child other than her own. That made me so sick in the stomach, because I knew my mother was not like that, and I lost my appetite for the food and started crying and wishing my mother was there to take us away from this wicked woman. We were not allowed to play around the house, so when we were done eating we had to go to our bedroom and stay there.

We would just stay there and hope things would get better, and that soon we would be out of there. I always kept my hope in Jehovah God and knew that someday I would see my mother again. The day that Aunty Umo's husband stayed home and insisted on seeing us, Aunty Umo pretended to be very nice to us and let us eat at her table, even asking us what we would like to eat. But when her husband was not around, we didn't get a choice of food; whatever was given to us was what we had to eat. Most days they would give us fried plantain to eat, sometimes it would be local street food.

We didn't know when our mother called, because Aunty Umo would usually refuse to let her talk to us. Whenever Aunty Umo let her talk to us, she made sure we stood right in front of her because she wanted to control what was being said. My mother told us that she had spoken to our Grand-aunty Kombaah, and that Aunty Kombaah was going to buy us tickets to get back to Liberia.

My mother told us that the people who worked on the plane would get us to Liberia, where we would then be picked up from the airport by our Grand-aunty Kombaah. We were not sure when that was going to be, so we kept living our normal abusive life in the house of Aunty Umo until the day we left. I remember a woman who was living at the house by the name of Challia, and she was always beating us for something, either because we put a hand on the wall or because we were running. I wanted to tell my mother how badly we were being treated, so one day, when no one was looking, I crept into Aunty Umo's bedroom so no one could see me or hear what I said, and I took the house phone that was in the room to make a call to my mother.

I did not have a number for my mother, but I was hoping that by dialing any number it would get to her and she would pick up the phone. Each time I dialled a number, the person on the other end would answer in French, and because I am unable to speak or understand French, I would hang up and dial another number. Unfortunately for me, Challia wanted to use the phone and realized that someone was on it, and that the call was coming from Aunty Umo's bedroom, so she decided to come and check.

When I heard her coming, I ran and hid myself under the bed, but I forgot to hang up the phone, so she came and found that the phone was still on. Challia said, "I know you are still in there so you had better come out, or else when I look for you and find you, you are not going to like what I will do to you." I had no choice but to come out from under the bed, because she said if I didn't, she would lock Aunty Umo's bedroom door with me in the room and wait until Aunty Umo got home before she opened it. When I got out from under the bed, I met Challia standing with a whip in her hand and she give me the beating of my life.

When Aunty Umo got home, she was told about my actions and she beat me badly, and punished me even further by not giving me food to eat the rest of the evening and I had to go to bed very hungry. I was told that if I ever got close to Aunty Umo's bedroom again to call my mother, that would be the day I wished I was never born. Aunty Umo was celebrating her son's birthday party and invited a lot of other rich kids to it, and we were not invited. We were asked to stay in our bedroom and to not come out. As we sat on the bedroom floor, we wished we were out there playing with the other kids and having something to eat.

Finally, it was time for us to return to Liberia—our Grand-aunty Kombaah had bought the tickets for us to return. The day Aunty Umo told us that we would be leaving in two days was one of the happiest days of my life. I remember her saying, "I know you people will forget about us when you return to Liberia and not even remember the way you people were taken care of when you were here." In my head I was saying, *Yeah, right, I will never forget the way we were treated so badly by our own relative.* The wait to leave was one of the longest two days of my life; I just could not wait until we got out of there.

# Chapter 9

# Our Return to Liberia: Another Year Without My Mother

The day came when it was time for us to leave. I was so happy I just could not wait to get out of there. It was very early in the morning when we left, and we were unable to tell Aunty Umo's kids that we were leaving. We got dropped off at the airport, where we were taken care of by the air hostesses until we arrived safe in Liberia. It was our first time travelling by plane and it was a fun experience for us. On the plane, we were given something to eat and drink. At first, it was a bit scary looking out the window, but later it became fun seeing the clouds in the sky.

When we got to the airport in Liberia, our Aunty Kulubaah came to pick us up. My mother Deborah was not there to pick us up, but anywhere away from Aunty Umo was better than staying with her. Aunty Kombaah picked us up and took us over to our grandmother Stuciah's house, where we were welcomed and felt at home. Our Aunty Sarafina was excited to show us to all her friends and to other relatives we didn't know we had. We settled in, but it was only two bedrooms with a place outside to shower.

There was no place to go to the toilet. It was a shock for us, because including my grandmother Stuciah and her boyfriend, kids, and grandkids, we were about twenty people living in a two-bedroom with a little space for dishes and a barrel for water, and that little space was known as the kitchen. My Aunty Wawanibo had her own bedroom and my grandmother had her own bedroom, so the little space used for the kitchen was where we slept at night, on the floor with sheets on the ground and no pillows to rest our heads.

We had to use our arms as pillows, and when they got numb we would switch to the next arm. We found ourselves doing that all night until we fell into a deep sleep. We got so used to sleeping that way that we just ended up putting our heads on the ground to sleep, because over time it got to feel comfortable.

There was another shocker for us when it was time to take a shower, because the place to shower was just an unfinished little space with no door for privacy, just a cloth used as a door. When the wind blew, the curtain would blow away, and if someone was standing by they could see us naked. There were also rocks on the ground to stand on, and we used a bucket to shower our skin.

During our shower, we would see worms coming from the ground. At my first experience with that I screamed and my grandmother Stuciah thought something happened to me.

She came running out, and when she realized it was just worms, she went and grabbed salt to kill them. When she put the salt on them they started jumping all over the place. For my grandmother Stuciah it was just worms, but for me it was my worst nightmare, because I hate worms with a passion and I kept saying to myself, *How I am going to survive this kind of life?*

Another shocker was when it came time to use the toilet; there was no place to urinate or poop. If you wanted to urinate you had to do it outside, and if you wanted to poop you had to poop in a plastic bag, and I was like, what? I was not used to pooping and looking at my own shit coming out, but I had to get used to it.

Therefore, when I went to poop, I would close my eyes for fear I might see something coming out that I didn't want to see. When a person was done pooping, they would put it in a corner, and when it got dark they would take it to where all garbage was deposited at the dump site. It was disgusting because it would stink so badly. You would have to carry everyone's poop when it was your turn to throw it away.

I didn't know that my great-grandmother Caba lived next door. The place they allowed us to poop was in an unfinished room right at the entrance of my great-grandmother Caba's back door, so one day while I was pooping I heard someone trying to come out and I quickly jumped up. Just then my Aunty Sarafina came to poop as well, and I told her someone was trying to open the door. That was when she told me it was my great-grandmother Caba. She told me to stay very quiet because my great-grandmother Caba hears everything, and if I made a sound she would hear me. My great-grandmother's name is Pearline, but everyone called her Caba—I think she got the name because she attended the Kingdom Hall of Jehovah's Witnesses as a baptized sister who went out to preach to people.

The first time I saw what my great-grandmother looked like, she came out and asked who was there, but I could not say anything. She came out to throw her dirty water in the unfinished room, and my Aunty Sarafina warned me to stay out of her way and watch where she threw the dirty water or else it would touch me. I tried to look in her room, but it was too dark and I couldn't see anything at all. I started to wonder how she could even see where she was going, and that was when my Aunty Sarafina told me that my great-grandmother Caba became blind when she was very young and was unable to see any of her grandkids or great-grandkids.

My Aunty Sarafina sat beside me and explained a lot of things that I should know, and things that go on that I am not allowed to talk about. I decided to take a closer look at my poop, and a fly came and sat on it and pooped on my poop, and when I looked at what the fly was doing, I realized that the fly laid eggs on my poop and its eggs were maggots, and that made me feel even more disgusted and gave me more reason not to ever open my eyes when I pooped. After learning a lot about some stuff I was unaware of, we wiped our butts with paper. I wasn't used to it, but my Aunty Sarafina showed me how to rub the paper together to make it soft. After I did that, I noticed a big difference using regular paper.

We went out to play, and in no time I had a lot of new friends to play with. It had been a few months and we had still heard nothing about our mother and whether or not she was doing OK. I began to worry, but I would always pray when I was alone that Jehovah God would keep her safe and to please bring her home.

One night, my Aunty Wawanibo decided she would have a fashion show and the winner would get a prize, and I like to win. My Aunty Wawanibo and grandmother Stuciah had me and my sister Yahgahbo wear bras, and they put cloth in them so we could have big make-believe breasts, and they tied pillows on our butts so we could have big make-believe butts. I won the competition, but my grandmother Stuciah suggested that my sister and Aunty Sarafina would not be happy, so we should all be considered winners. My Aunty Sarafina is my grandmother's last child and her favourite amongst all her other children, because she was in love with Sarafina's father and will always be in love with him.

My grandmother Stuciah had nine kids by six men, not a very fine example for any of her kids, but no matter who you are and what you become your children will always love you for who you are. There was a fight competition between Sarafina and me because she would pick on me, so my Aunty Wawanibo got mad one day and said we should fight. I am not sure where all my strength came from, but I knocked my Aunty Sarafina down and sat on top of her and started to slap her face and told her to apologize for all the times she made my life miserable. She refused, so I kept slapping her until my grandmother came and said that I shouldn't slap her face, but her butt instead.

Slapping her butt would not make her feel anything because her butt was too big. My Aunty Wawanibo had enough of us fighting and parted us, and from that day onward I was never bullied by her again, because she now knew that if she ever tried, there would be a fight between us.

It was time for school to start, so my Grand-aunty Kombaah give my grandmother Stuciah money to register us in a Catholic school called St. Mary, because she could not afford to put the three of us in the international school we once attended when we were with our parents.

Grand-aunty Kombaah re-registered Yahgahbo at the Mounsorado International School because she could only afford to send one person, but I was happy to be attending the same school as my Aunty Sarafina. My grandmother Stuciah didn't want Sarafina to be left behind, so she registered her with me in Grade Two. What I didn't know was that Sarafina was very dull and didn't like school very much, because her mother didn't encourage her to do so. Sarafina was failing badly in Grade Two; during exams she would even grab my exam papers off my desk to copy and I would be very mad at her.

One day, she was caught by the teacher and sent to the principal's office, and my Grandmother Stuciah was sent for. After that day, my grandmother Stuciah decided that my Uncle Bodosak would be our home tutor. But even when he was teaching us, Sarafina still would not remember anything she was taught, and she had a problem reading. Uncle Bodosak usually gave us a hand whipping if we didn't remember what was being taught, so I studied harder. However, my Aunty Sarafina would not study at all, and when it came time for tutoring, she did not know what was being said so Uncle Bodosak would whip her.

One day, my grandmother Stuciah heard Sarafina crying, and she said that if Sarafina did not want to learn it was not necessary, and she took Sarafina out of the study class. Sarafina's grades continued to drop, and when it came to completing the school year she was asked to repeat Grade Two, and I was promoted to Grade Three. When school closed, my Grand-aunty Kombaah came to give presents to those who passed and when I was asked what it was I wanted for my present, I told her that I would like to take my whole summer and go work with her at her clothing boutique.

My Grand-aunty Kombaah always loved and cared for her mother very much. She agreed to take me to spend my summer vacation with her, but Chakakuka, Yahgahbo, and Aunty Sarafina were not happy. I didn't want to spend another minute delaying before my Grand-aunty Kombaah changed her mind, so I ran into my grandmother's place, grabbed most of my clothing, and was ready to leave.

Aunty Kombaah took me to her place, and there I met my grand-cousins Xenna and Edward. There was a girl living with them, her name was Maymay and she was said to be a relative to my Grand-aunty's husband, Uncle Edward. When night fell, everyone wanted me to sleep with them on their bed, but they didn't know that I slept very wild and at that time I would sometimes pee the bed. All night I kicked in my sleep, making it hard for them to sleep, so they told me to sleep on a blanket they put on the ground.

The next morning came, and no one wanted me to share their bed with them again. From then on, at night-time, they would put some bedsheets and a blanket on the floor for me to sleep on, because if it got wet from my pee it could easily be washed, plus I wouldn't have to kick anyone while I slept, because it would only be me sleeping alone on the floor. Once I got familiarized with the environment, it was time for me to start my summer job at my Grand-aunty Kombaah's boutique.

The first day of my summer job, Aunty Kombaah told me she would give me a ride to her boutique, but after that I had to find my own way if I was really serious about keeping the job. That would also mean going to bed very early so I wouldn't be late for work. I have a very good, photographic memory, so I remembered the location, but I did not know how far it was until my second day of work. That was when I realized it was more than a hundred blocks away.

My passion to work at that very young age kept me very motivated, and nothing was going to stop me. When my Grand-aunty Kombaah saw how determined I was to keep my summer job and that I didn't mind the distance, she told me the job was mine, but because I was very young and it wasn't right for her to give me money at that age, she told me to pick something I liked from the boutique, and at the end of the month she would give it to me as my pay. The very first thing I picked was a pearl necklace set in a beautiful box.

It had a necklace, a bracelet, and an earring, and each day when I was at work, I would look at it with admiration and I could not wait for the day it would be all mine. Sometimes, my Grand-aunty Kombaah would send me on many errands in one day, and they would be many miles away, but I would still not complain because I had a passion for what I was doing.

When at home with my Grand-aunty Kombaah and her family, I would often get sad because it would remind me of the family I once had, and not knowing how my mother was doing made me even more sad.

Maymay would be the one to comfort me and tell me that everything was going to be OK, and that I shouldn't worry much. As for my Grand-cousin Xenna, she would not even want to hang out with me, because at the time we had no more money and I was not her type. She would only want to hang out with her father's rich friend's kids, but Maymay would always tell me to put my mouth where my hand can reach—meaning when you are poor you should only try to hang out with those who are poor as well, that way you won't feel hurt or rejected. I became friends with a

Lebanese girl by the name of Aleyna, who was fifteen years old. I did not know that girls that young got married. We were friends and became close; her family knew me, but I did not know that her family was arranging for her to get married at that young age.

Each time I visited her, she would show me how her parents' business worked, and we would sit and chat. I did not get much time in the day to spend with her because I had to return to my Grand-aunty Kombaah's clothing store. At one point, it had been a few days since I had last seen Aleyna, so I decided to go and look for her. When I found her, she looked a bit sad, but I did not know what the problem was.

One time, I went to visit Aleyna, and her family told me that she was travelling but didn't tell me that they already married her off to an older guy. When Aleyna returned, I went to visit her, and her mother told me that she wasn't feeling well and that she was lying down in the office, but it was OK for me to go in and see her.

She had a fever and was feeling very cold, but the air conditioning was on high. I thought they must have been crazy to have it on so high while this girl had a fever. What I didn't know was that she was pregnant. I did not know what a pregnant girl looked like. I chatted with Aleyna for a bit, and then I had to go get food for my Grand-aunty Kombaah. I told Aleyna that I would be back to visit her, but with so much work to do for my Grand-aunty Kombaah, I lost track of how long it was since I last visited her.

The next time I saw her, it had been a while and her stomach was very big. That was when she told me she was having a baby, and I cried because she was still a child. I couldn't stop crying and thinking about how evil her family was to do that to her. I spent a bit more time with her and asked her lots of questions about what life was going to be like for her, and she told me that once she had the baby, she would no longer be able to see me, as she would now be with her husband taking care of her kid. I cried some more and did not know what to say or do; it was almost like I wanted to rescue her from her family but all I could do was wish that her life could be better.

Grand-aunty Kombaah had this man working for her at her clothing store by the name of Pitet. He was a full-time worker and I was just a part-time worker. Grand-aunty Kombaah had to travel for business, so that meant I had to walk myself to her store and back every day. When Grand-aunty Kombaah was not around, Pitet would tell me that he was going to get some things for the store and he would be gone for hours. I would be in the store alone serving customers and giving them their change when they made a purchase.

The customers were surprised at how good I was at giving them their exact change and also receiving the right amount of payment for things they were interested in. Grand-aunty Kombaah was not gone for long, and when she returned she heard a lot of good stuff about how I had been working hard and how accurate I was when it came to receiving payments or giving change. Grand-aunty Kombaah was pleased and told me that I should take the pearl necklace set as my payment for a job well done.

I also told Grand-aunty Kombaah how Pitet would leave me alone most times to care for the store. She told him that I was much too young to be left alone in the store. She also told him that anyone could have come into the store, knowing that I was alone, and steal stuff, including the money.

I did not get to know much about my Grand-cousin Xenna, because she was always away visiting one of her rich friends or another rich family member. I got to know Maymay a bit more, because whenever I was done helping out at the store, I would come home and help her around the house with either the dishes or the sweeping, or I would help to get the dinner ready.

It was time for me to return to my grandmother Stuciah's house to prepare to go back to school. Though I was going to miss my time spent with my Grand-aunty Kombaah, it was time for me to return, and it had been a while since I last saw Chakakuka and Yahgahbo. My summer vacation was long over, and I was back at my grandmother's place, and they were all awaiting my return to warn me not to think I was special because I spent time at my Grand-aunty Kombaah's place. They reminded me I was back with them now, and I had to do what they all did. My Grand-aunty Kombaah gave me a lot of stuff, including food, for the time I stayed at her place and helped her, but at my grandmother's place, none of that was mine anymore. I went back to pooping in plastic bags and showering outside. I wish I never lived there. I had no choice but to wait until my mother returned to take us out of there.

My Aunty Sarafina knew everyone in her area, and started to take me around and introduce me to some of her friends. There were boys asking my aunty who the new girl was, and she would tell them that I was her sister's daughter, and her sister wasn't there but soon she would come for her kids. When it came to evening time, my Aunty Sarafina would take me to a place called a video club; it is a tight little space where people go to watch movies. Most times she would get boys to get us in, and sometimes it would be boys that worked at the video club whom she knew. My grandmother Stuciah was such a don't-care grandmother that we were allowed to do whatever we wanted.

She would send us to buy her beer and share it with us, including my little boy cousin called Baby Tukar. I know you are wondering what kind of grandmother would do this, but to us, she was the coolest grandmother ever. She would talk to us about her past relationships and about men being cheaters. Sometimes she would ask if any of us had a boyfriend; I would tell her no because I didn't know what it meant to have a boyfriend, and I wasn't even thinking about it. I started to get to know more friends, and every girl had a boyfriend or some kind of crush, so I thought maybe it would be wise to have a crush or a boyfriend, too.

There was this person at the time who would hang out with all the little boys in the community, so I thought he was little, too. I started to have a crush on him, and he had a crush on me. When I asked how old he was, he said he was twelve, so each time he would go and get water from the well with the other boys in the community I would say I was going to shower outside. When I saw him coming, I would grab my towel and try to hide my nakedness. Sometimes we would all go get water from the well with other girls and boys. It went on for a while; I even visited him at his sister's house because he used to stay with her, and I would sit and watch him clean and cook.

One day while I was helping my grandmother Stuciah with her sewing, she asked me, "So, who's your boyfriend or your crush?" I said that the boy's name was Garmu and that he was twelve years old. My grandmother Stuciah said, "Garmu who?" She was very surprised, because she knew how old he was and she would never let that happen. She then told me that Garmu didn't tell me the truth about how old he was; she told me that Garmu was not twelve years old, that he was a twenty-six-year-old man and that she was going over to his sister's place to disgrace him in front of everyone and tell people the kind of foolish guy he was.

My grandmother Stuciah left her sewing and wore very short pants to go fight Garmu. She went over with a frying pan in one hand and a cooking spoon in the other. As she walked over to where Garmu lived, she knocked the cooking spoon and frying pan together to make a lot of noise to get everyone's attention to what was going on. When she finally got to where Garmu lived, the compound was packed with nosy people wanting to know what was going on.

My grandmother Stuciah was screaming for Garmu to come out so she could beat him, but Garmu was so scared of what would happen that he didn't come outside, so my grandmother Stuciah waited until his sister returned from work, and she explained what happened and how Garmu was trying to be sexual with her granddaughter who is just a child. Garmu's sister Olua felt very sad, and told my grandmother Stuciah how sorry she was for what happened and that she would take serious action on her brother.

Later that evening, when Garmu's sister's husband returned from work, she told him what Garmu did and Garmu got the beating of his life. I felt so sad for Garmu because he got beaten badly, and my grandmother Stuciah warned that the day she ever sees Garmu speak to me would be the day she would call the police to arrest him and put him in jail. Since then, Garmu made sure he stayed far away from me, and it was good for my own protection because I was still a child I didn't realize the danger of having an adult lie about how old they were just to be around a child.

It was not long after the Garmu incident that I started getting followed by this older light-skinned person. Each time my grandmother Stuciah or Aunty Wawanibo would send me to some Ghanaian person's shop to buy something, this person would try to talk to me and I would get scared and hurry home. It came to the point that he started coming around the house of my grandmother Stuciah, so I got really scared and I told my Aunty Wawanibo about him: an older guy who kept trying to talk to me and follow me.

My Aunty Wawanibo got very mad and took along some of my uncles to go and meet this guy to give him a warning. When they got to where he lived, the place became overcrowded because everyone wanted to know what was going on with all the noise and a possible fight.

After what had been happening, my Aunty Wawanibo got very scared for me, and said that from then on she would need to keep her eyes on me. She didn't want anything bad happening to me, or my mother blaming her for not taking good care of me. That meant no more staying out late with my Aunty Sarafina at the video club or hanging late with some friends. My grandmother Stuciah allowed us to be out very late and pretty much do whatever we wanted, but my Aunty Wawanibo said it was a no in her book, and sometimes getting away from my aunty required help from my grandmother Stuciah.

Every little girl had a boy they had a crush on, so I needed one too, but I was so little I could not tell the difference between having a good crush and a bad crush. My other Aunty Peyeeh, although young, was dating a Lebanese guy name Farrdeeh, and in the compound where he lived there was a mixed-race boy named Zouseefh. He was older than me and lived there with his parents. Each time Aunty Peyeeh would ask my Aunty Sarafina and me to come visit her, it was always a pleasure because I wanted to spy on Youseefh.

I had such a mad crush on him it didn't matter how old I was, I just wanted to be with him, and each time he noticed me, it made my day and I would get so happy. I told my Aunty Sarafina how I felt about Youseefh, so one day when we were asked by Aunty Peyeeh who we had a crush on, my Aunty Sarafina told Aunty Peyeeh who her crush was. It was a boy who lived in the next compound from Aunty Peyeeh's house. She told Aunty Peyeeh that my crush was Youseefh.

One day while helping Aunty Peyeeh, she said that she wanted to grab something from Youseefh's mother, who lived just below Aunty Peyeeh, and that I should come with her. When we got there, Aunty Peyeeh asked Youseefh's mother where Youseefh was, and his mother told Aunty Peyeeh that he was not home.

While I was a bit disappointed, Aunty Peyeeh had a surprise for me. She told Youseefh's mother that I had a crush on her son, and his mother got a big smile on her face and said she would tell her son when he got home. After my Aunty Peyeeh got what she went for, we left and went back upstairs. Just at that time, I heard the compound gate open; it was

Youseefh, and my heart started to pound because I knew he was about to find out that I liked him.

While Youseefh and his mother sat to chat, I heard her say to him, "The woman, Peyeeh from upstairs, came with a little wife for you, but you were not here to meet her. But I am sure when you see her, you will like her because she is beautiful. She is upstairs at Peyeeh's place." I felt butterflies in my stomach, and I was not sure how to leave Aunty Peyeeh's place because I knew he was going to be looking out for me to see what I looked like.

When it was time for me to leave, I came downstairs and there was no one there so I happily walked toward the gate, but Youseefh was standing outside with a friend, and when I walked past them, I didn't say a word, I just kept walking. I could hear them talking, and Youseefh was telling his friend that he learned from his mother that I liked him, and although the friend tried to tell Youseefh that I was much too young, he said to his friend that it didn't matter.

After visiting a few times at Aunty Peyeeh and her boyfriend Farrdeeh's place, I asked my Aunty Sarafina to please take me there so I could meet Youseefh to see if he liked me, and my Aunty Sarafina agreed, but she made me promise to take her to her crush, too, and I also agreed. We took Yahgahbo to the video club and told her we would be right back. But I made a mistake: I told her I was going to meet up with Youseefh and that I would not be long. So off to Youseefh's we went, and fortunately for me he was home.

We got to his house, and as soon as his mother saw me, she said, "Is that my son's wife?" I asked if Youseefh was home and she said yes, and that he was in his room, so my Aunty Sarafina waited for me in the living room and I went into Youseefh's room looking for him. When I entered the room, it was as if he was expecting me. We talked a little, and just when he was about to kiss me, I heard the voice of my Aunty Wawanibo scream for us to bring our butts out of the house, and she started pounding the gate.

Apparently, she went over to the video club to look for us because it was getting late and she didn't like the fact that our grandmother Stuciah allowed us to do whatever we wanted, including staying out late at night at a very young age, so when Yahgahbo told her we went to Youseefh's place she came to beat us up, because she said we were too young to be around boys that were older than us and to be out that late.

I quickly left Youseefh in his room and went running out to my Aunty Sarafina, and we told Youseefh's mother goodbye. We were scared as hell, because my Aunty Wawanibo was going crazy outside, screaming about how when she got her hands on us we were going to regret what we did. My Aunty Sarafina and I weren't sure who was going to go out first, because Aunty Wawanibo was standing at the gate with a whip in her hand. I told Sarafina to go first, and when she did, Aunty Wawanibo started to whip her, and I ran past them to my grandmother Stuciah. As I ran, I could hear Aunty Wawanibo screaming, "You can run but you can't hide, because when I get home I will still whip you, and your grandmother Stuciah can't stop me." But I didn't care, I just kept running.

When I got home, I explained to my grandmother Stuciah all that happened and she said to me, "Just wait, Wawanibo won't touch you when she gets home. I will tell her that you are fast asleep and that whatever discipline she wants to give you can wait till the morning."

It was not long until my Aunty Sarafina came home crying and telling my grandmother Stuciah that her sister Wawanibo had beat her up because we went to visit one of our friends. My grandmother Stuciah was mad about that, and when my Aunty Wawanibo came home, my grandmother Stuciah told her not to put her hands on my Aunty Sarafina anymore. My Aunty Wawanibo said to my grandmother Stuciah, "It's up to you if you want your daughter Sarafina to be spoiled, but as for my sister's daughter Arnelle, I will discipline her the way I like until my sister Deborah returns, because if I sit here and let her daughter get spoiled, she's going to put the blame on me for not being there for her child."

So that night, my Aunty Wawanibo wanted me to come out so she could beat me up, but my grandmother Stuciah said to her that I was fast asleep and that she cannot discipline me. My grandmother Stuciah told her to wait until the next day if she liked, but she would not let my Aunty Wawanibo wake me from my sleep just to beat me up. My Aunty Wawanibo was mad about it and said that even if I sleep for a year, she would still beat me when I woke up.

The next day, my Aunty Wawanibo's childhood friend Debe came to visit her, and she told her everything that been going on in my grandmother

Stuciah's house. Aunty Wawanibo told Debe how my grandmother Stuciah allowed us to do whatever we wanted, even allowed us to come home very late at night. Then Debe asked where I was, and Aunty Wawanibo told her I was out playing, so they called for me to come inside and I was questioned.

Debe said to me, "So, you following Sarafina and misbehaving, right? When your mother Deborah return and hear all of this, you will see what she will do to you." I was scared and told myself to behave, because I did not want my mother mad at me.

Life went on as usual, and when it was my turn to do dishes, I would wash them on time. My Aunty Wawanibo always had a new boyfriend; some were European and others were African, but she had one African boyfriend she used to like very much and he worked in the government of Liberia. He was a married man with kids. They spent a lot of time together, and even my grandmother Stuciah knew him. Sometimes, my great-grandmother Caba came to visit my grandmother Stuciah, and because Wawanibo's room shared the same wall as my great-grandmother Caba's, my great-grandmother could hear everything that went on in my Aunty Wawanibo's bedroom.

She would say to Aunty Wawanibo, "How many men you allowing to get in your big old hole?" and Wawanibo would get very mad and tell her mother Stuciah, "Mama, please tell your mother not to put her mouth in my business." Each time my Aunty Wawanibo and her childhood friend Debe were together, they would talk about sex and different guys. The first time I ever heard that people could have sex in their ass was when Aunty Wawanibo told her friend Debe that one European guy she had been seeing asked to have sex with her in her ass, and she said she tried it but it was too uncomfortable. She said when the man took his dick out there was poop on it.

I was shocked at what I heard, but with the kind of conversation my Aunty Wawanibo had with her friend Debe there were no surprises; sometimes they would even gossip about my grandmother Stuciah, so she started giving us money to get any information about what was being said about her. One day while Aunty Wawanibo was talking to Debe, Yahgahbo and I were eavesdropping at my Aunty Wawanibo's door. We had our heads down and our butts up in the air and didn't see Aunty Wawanibo open up her bedroom door and catch us.

When we noticed Aunty Wawanibo standing there, it was too late to run away and hide. She said, "Since you people want to hear adult conversation, I am going to bring you in my room so you both can hear it good." We started crying and didn't want to hear it anymore, but she took us into her room and told her friend Debe what she caught us doing. Debe said, "Wow, so you guys want to listen to us? Right, sit and listen good," and they started talking about sex and everything else and we didn't want to hear it.

Aunty Wawanibo beat us up and sent us out of her room, and since that day we remembered not to bend down in front of her door. What we planned to do was go around the house and sit under her bedroom window and pretend to be playing. When she noticed us playing under her window and listening to what she was saying, she told us she no longer wanted us playing under her window, and said that if she finds us ever doing it again she would whip us.

My Aunty Peyeeh took money from her Lebanese boyfriend and started building parts of the unfinished building my great-grandmother owned as part of her own space. When it was completed, Aunty Peyeeh said if it was OK for us, my Aunty Sarafina, my sister Yahgahbo, and I could sleep there whenever we wanted to, and to make sure to take good care of it and allow no one to steal her things, but my Aunty Wawanibo wasn't happy about that. She said we were too young for Aunty Peyeeh to allow us to sleep on the other side of the building alone by ourselves.

My grandmother Stuciah allowed my Aunty Sarafina to sleep on the other side of the building, whereas Aunty Wawanibo insisted Yahgahbo and I slept over in her bedroom on the floor.

When we could not take sleeping on the hard floor any more, we insisted that we would like to sleep in our Aunty Peyeeh's new place, and my grandmother Stuciah said we could sleep there. Aunty Wawanibo was determined not to give up on making sure that we were not up very late each night; she wanted to make sure we were in bed by 10 p.m., but all our friends were done their work and showered after 10:00, and that is when they all went out to chat and tell stories.

Aunty Wawanibo was totally against us being out late at night, so we would leave the radio on in the room and turn the lights off and lock the door. When we heard her coming, we would hide and the other kids would tell her we were not outside. When she returned to her room, we would sit back down and laugh and chat with our friends all night, but what we didn't realize was that Aunty Wawanibo loved to read her love books late at night, and most times she would hear us talking outside and laughing.

One fine night when we thought we were having a good time, Aunty Wawanibo had her own plans for us. She did not make a sound; she came out with her belt and whipped us up really well. There was no escaping her because we did not know she was coming.

I became Aunty Wawanibo's personal assistant and my job required me to clean her bedroom, do her laundry, go to the market for her, prepare the meal she was going to cook, do her manicures and pedicures, be her hair stylist, be her errand girl, and the list goes on and on. Becoming the errand girl for Aunty Wawanibo limited me from spending time with my friends. Sometimes my Aunty Sarafina would tell us to run away and go to a different community to play with some of her other friends. Aunty Wawanibo would call me, and if I did not answer because I wasn't home, she would call me into her bedroom when I returned and ask me questions, and if she didn't trust the answer, she would take off her belt and beat me up.

Sometimes my grandmother Stuciah would knock on Aunty Wawanibo's door and get me out, and Aunty Wawanibo would get mad and say my grandmother Stuciah was spoiling us. One day, my Aunty Sarafina said we should go watch a live basketball game at the basketball stadium, Sport Commission. My grandmother Stuciah gave us some money to buy our tickets and food and drinks. We didn't have much for decent clothes, so my grandmother Stuciah suggested we borrow some from my Aunty Wawanibo's closet to wear but told us to return on time so that we could put it back.

We agreed; Sarafina, Yahgahbo, and I went into Aunty Wawanibo's closet and started to select what we wanted to wear. Aunty Wawanibo had a purple silk-like flirt skirt I always liked, and I chose that with her white platform slippers and one of her white tops. The skirt, top, and slippers were way too big for me, so my grandmother Stuciah use diaper pins to adjust the waist of the skirt, and she rolled up the arms of the blouse. The slippers had a big space left at the back because they didn't fit me.

My grandmother told me not to worry, no one would ever notice how big the slippers were because the skirt was long enough to cover them. She wanted me to put the blouse into the skirt, so I did, but not for long. As soon as Yahgahbo and my Aunty Sarafina were ready and we left the house to take a taxi, I pulled the blouse out and tied it over my belly button. We took the taxi to downtown Monrovia and got out at the Sport Commission. We paid for our taxi and got out to find there was a huge line-up.

We waited in line to pay for our tickets, and got in just in time to find the right seats so we would be able to watch the game at a close distance. While we were seating ourselves to watch the games, some boys came and sat next to us and offered to buy us food and drinks.

At first I refused their offer, but my Aunty Sarafina said it would be good for us to accept, that way we would be able to keep the money my grandmother Stuciah gave us to buy food and drinks. I agreed, so my Aunty Sarafina and Yahgahbo followed two of the guys to get the food and drinks for us as I waited to make sure that our seats were not taken. One of the boys stayed behind as well, because he was interested in talking to me.

He asked me what my name was, and I responded Arnelle with an attitude that said I was not there to talk to him. The boy told me that his name was Marl and that he was interested in making me his girlfriend. He said that his family lived a good life and that he attended one of the most expensive schools and had money enough to buy me whatever I wanted. I told him that I wasn't interested in him buying me anything, but Marl wasn't giving up. He continued to watch the basketball game while he waited for his friends to return, along with my sister and aunty.

When my Aunty Sarafina and Yahgahbo returned, they seemed happy, and brought food and drinks for us. One of Marl's friends was talking to my sister and the other friend was talking to my Aunty Sarafina. The basketball game went well and our team won, so Marl and his friends decided they wanted to go to an entertainment spot called Monte Carlo, and they asked us to come along. I told my Aunty Sarafina that we should go home before we got into bigger trouble, but she said that my Aunty Wawanibo wouldn't be coming home until the next day.

My Aunty Sarafina wanted to go with Marl and his friends, so Yahgahbo and I ended up going along with them. When we got to Monte Carlo, there were lots of video games to play and they sold food and drinks. Though I wasn't sure how to play the video games, Marl insisted on teaching me.

Yahgahbo was busy chatting with one of the boys and my Aunty Sarafina was having drinks with another. Marl started to get closer to me in a way that made me uncomfortable, so I told my Aunty Sarafina that we should get going, but she said I needed to be more relaxed and that the boys were nice. I told her that I did not like the way Marl was advancing on me, but she told me that he told her that he really liked me. I told her that I was not interested in Marl and would like to go home. She told me to wait a little bit, as she was talking to one of his friends; when she was done then we would go.

As I waited for my Aunty Sarafina, Marl tried to talk to me again, but I ignored him. It was getting a bit late, so my Aunty Sarafina decided we should get going home before it got hard for us to find a taxi. Marl and his friends made sure we got a taxi, but I did not know that my Aunty Sarafina wrote down our address so that Marl could come and look for me.

As we walked home, we talked about our day, the basketball game, and the boys we met. We were unaware that Aunty Wawanibo had come home early that day and had found out from my grandmother Stuciah that we went to watch the basketball game. She also found out that her clothes were missing, and when she asked my grandmother Stuciah what happened to them, she denied knowing anything about it. Aunty Wawanibo knew we wore her clothes, and she was just waiting to catch us.

We got closer to my grandmother Stuciah's house, and there was Aunty Wawanibo, sitting in front of the house waiting for us. Before we could run, it was too late. Aunty Wawanibo said to us, "Don't you guys dare run, because if you do, you are not going to like what I will do to the three of you."

Shaking, the three of us got into my grandmother's house, but unfortunately for us, my grandmother Stuciah had gone to visit a friend and we were unsure when she would be home. Aunty Wawanibo saw her clothes on us, and it upset her even more. She told us to take her clothes off and we did, leaving us in just our panties. Aunty Wawanibo took her belt and started beating us one at a time. She beat us badly and made us promise never to touch or wear her clothes again. Before Aunty Wawanibo could get to my Aunty Sarafina, my grandmother Stuciah got home and told Aunty Wawanibo that she would not allow Aunty Wawanibo to put her hands on Sarafina.

My grandmother Stuciah said that if she had been home, she wouldn't have allowed my Aunty Wawanibo to beat us up like that. Aunty Wawanibo said my grandmother Stuciah should keep Sarafina away from everything that belonged to her, and if Sarafina ever touched any of her stuff, that would be the day she and my grandmother would get into a fight. My grandmother Stuciah told my Aunty Wawanibo that the day she ever put her hands on Sarafina would be the day my Aunty Wawanibo should get ready to fight her.

After that day, Aunty Wawanibo always kept a watchful eye on my sister and me. She was always sending me to buy something or to do something for her. One day, Aunty Wawanibo sent me to buy laundry soap for her to wash her dirty clothes, but on the way I dropped her money and it was stolen. I tried for a couple hours to retrace my steps to see if I could find it, but no matter how hard I looked I could not find it, so I decided to return home and tell Aunty Wawanibo that the money for her soap got lost. When I got home to my grandmother's house, I told Aunty Wawanibo that her money went missing, and that I tried so hard to find it but I just couldn't. Aunty Wawanibo told me that if I knew what was good for me, I would make sure to give her the money for her soap.

Aunty Wawanibo told me the money she gave me was the only money she had left to buy soap to wash her clothes, and since I told her I could not find it I should go into her room and bring her belt. When I brought her belt, she beat me up with it until it was in pieces. She told me that I should leave my grandmother Stuciah's house and not come back until I brought her the money for her soap.

Since I didn't know how to get her back her money, I decided to sit on a big rock that was right in front my grandmother Stuciah's house. From morning until very late afternoon, I was given nothing to eat and nothing to drink. My grandmother Stuciah wasn't at home and there was no one to save me from Aunty Wawanibo. While sitting there thinking what to do and where to go, Aunty Wawanibo came out in front of my grandmother's and saw me sitting on the rock, and said that it looked like I didn't do anything to look for her money. She grabbed me by my clothes and started slapping, kicking, and punching me.

Aunty Wawanibo kicked me in my stomach. People around tried to tell her to stop, but she said it was none of their business, that it was a family problem. People who didn't want to deal with her walked away, but a man who was selling things in his wheelbarrow saw the way my Aunty Wawanibo was beating me up and got extremely angry, and asked her, "What wrong did this little girl do for you to beat her up like this?" Aunty Wawanibo responded by saying, "You better go and sell whatever it is you are selling and mind your own business."

The guy said to Aunty Wawanibo, "It looks like this girl's mother is not around and you are one of those bad family members that mistreats a child. If you ever put your hands on this girl again, I will beat the shit out of you." Seeing how mad the guy was scared Aunty Wawanibo.

Aunty Wawanibo was so scared of what the guy was going to do to her that she said to me, "You are so lucky that fool got himself involved, but I am not done with you yet." She left and went back into my grandmother Stuciah's house. I went back to sitting on the rock waiting for my grandmother Stuciah to get home. Aunty Wawanibo cooked and forbade my Aunty Sarafina and my sister Yahgahbo from sharing their food with me, and told them that if they gave me something to eat, she would beat them up. I remember my Aunty Sarafina hiding some of her food and sneaking out to give it to me to eat.

My grandmother Stuciah got home from her outing, saw me sitting on the rock, and asked me what I was doing there looking all beat up. I told her what Aunty Wawanibo did to me, and she said, "Follow me into the house and let me see if she dares to put her hands on you again. She's not going to like my reaction." Holding my hand, my grandmother took me into the house, and when Aunty Wawanibo saw me, she said, "What are you doing in here? I thought I told you not to come in here." My grandmother Stuciah responded to her by saying, "This is her grandmother's house, and she has the right to be in here."

My grandmother Stuciah told Aunty Wawanibo that she was no longer allowed to put her hands on me, because I wasn't given to her to take care of, so she had no right to punish me. For once, I said to myself, *Thank God*

*I am free from the hands of this woman.* Aunty Wawanibo was so mad she said to my grandmother Stuciah, "OK, I will have nothing to do with her anymore, but if something ever happens to her, you are going to be the one responsible." My grandmother Stuciah said, "Just leave her alone, nothing is going to happen to her. Every little thing this girl does you beat her up for; I am sick and tired of it." With the help of my grandmother Stuciah, I was now a free girl.

Now that I was free from Aunty Wawanibo's control, I could hang out more with my Aunty Sarafina and other friends. My Aunty Sarafina knew every avenue in her community and a lot of other kids. She introduced a lot of her friends to me, and soon I became known. My brother Chakakuka had his own friends in the area who he hung around with.

We had a friend, Tonney, whose father was Lebanese and whose mother was Liberian, but he lived with his stepmother Nuna and their father Mr. Jamer. Tonney and his sister Tamara had a lot of freedom after their stepmother Nuna left for America to stay. Tonney and Tamara lived alone with their father, who was always busy at work giving them the freedom to bring friends over and do whatever the hell they wanted. My Aunty Wawanibo did not like the fact that we started to hang out with Tonney and Tamara, because she said they had no restrictions and were living the way they pleased.

That did not stop us from visiting with Tamara and her brother Tonney, and yes, at their home there was lots of freedom because their father was not home. One Saturday, we went to visit them. When we got there, they had planned to go to the beach with their friends. We wanted to go with them but we did not have any swimming wear at the time, so Tamara lent hers to my sister, Aunty Sarafina, and me. As for my brother Chakakuka, he borrowed one of Tonney's short swimming pants and we all got ready and went to the beach.

Excitedly, we all headed to the beach, and when we got there we were asked to pay before getting in, but we had no money so Tamara paid for us all. We got in and settled ourselves to go for a swim. Right when we all started having fun, we heard a voice from behind us as we walked past a table with group of people seated at it. It said, "What are you guys doing here?" Upon hearing the voice, we knew it was Aunty Wawanibo, but it was too late to hide.

We stopped and greeted her and her friends. Shaking, we told her that we came to the beach with Tamara and Tonney. Surprisingly, Aunty Wawanibo told us to be careful and have fun, and to make sure to get back home early. But it was all pretend, because when we got home, she had already told our grandmother Stuciah that she saw us at the beach, and that some older Lebanese men were around Tamara and her friends and that our association with Tamara was not safe. We told our grandmother Stuciah that though it was true that we went to the beach with Tamara and her friends, we were not around her when she and her friends chatted with the Lebanese men.

Our grandmother Stuciah told us that the next time we wanted to go to the beach with Tamara, we should ask her first before going, that way she would be aware of our whereabouts. We said OK, that the next time we wanted to go we would ask her. Aunty Wawanibo got mad at our grandmother Stuciah's response and said that she was spoiling us, and that the day something happened to us it would be our grandmother to blame. Our grandmother Stuciah responded that nothing was going to happen to us and that she should allow us a bit of freedom.

Visiting Tamara and her brother Tonney became our new favourite thing. Whenever we were done helping our grandmother at the home, we would leave and go to visit Tamara and Tonney, because at their house we could eat whatever we wanted without restrictions. My Aunty Wawanibo came home one day and realized we were not at home, and when she asked about us, my grandmother told her that we had gone to Tamara's place.

Tamara wanted us to go to the beach but was scared that Aunty Wawanibo would find out, so we decided to tell my grandmother Stuciah that we were going to the video club to watch a movie, so we needed her to give us money. The money my grandmother Stuciah gave us was not enough.

My Aunty Sarafina did not want us to follow Tamara to the beach and have to beg her to get us in and beg her to buy us food, so my Aunty Sarafina came up with an idea. She knew where my grandmother Stuciah hid all her money, so she said that when she went out to take her bath, she would take the money that was hidden in the Bible.

My Aunty Sarafina's master plan included telling my Uncle Bodosak that my grandmother Stuciah wanted him to thread her sewing machine by the time she was finished her bath. My Uncle Bodosak believed my Aunty Sarafina without confirming with my grandmother Stuciah, and went to thread the needle of the sewing machine. The minute he entered our grandmother's bedroom, we left the room so that my grandmother would suspect him of being the one who stole her money.

It wasn't long before my grandmother Stuciah returned to her bedroom and saw my Uncle Bodosak about to leave her room. She said to him, "I just hope you haven't stolen my last money that I have kept in this room." Bodosak asked what she meant, and said that he had no idea of what money she was talking about. My grandmother Stuciah said to my Uncle Bodosak, "I got five hundred dollars in my room, and if I check and do not see it, I will make sure you give me back my money."

My grandmother Stuciah told my Uncle Bodosak not to go anywhere until she checked for her money. With this argument going on, my Aunty Sarafina hid the five hundred dollars in the dirty laundry basket just in case my grandmother was smart enough to search us. Bodosak swore he had nothing to do with my grandmother Stuciah's money, and when my grandmother checked, her money was gone so she blamed Bodosak for it.

She grabbed Bodosak and started beating him for stealing her money and threatened to sell all his things to replace it. I tried to tell my Aunty Sarafina to return the money, but she said that it was too late and that if we do give her the money, we would not have enough money to go to the beach, and we would be in big trouble with my grandmother.

I listened to my Aunty Sarafina, and off to Tamara's we went so that we could all go to the beach. When we got to Tamara's place they were just about to leave, so we got there just in time. Tamara said she almost left us behind because she did not want to get to the beach late. We all got in the taxi and to the beach we went. At the beach, Tamara said to us, "I hope you guys got your own money because my money is not enough to get all of you in."

My Aunty Sarafina said to Tamara, "Don't worry about us, we can get ourselves in." We went into the beach and started to have a lot of fun swimming. My Aunty Sarafina bought us something to drink and some roasted meat. The beach had a lagoon connected to the ocean, so we decided to swim in it. In the lagoon, there were lots of people swimming but some parts were very deep, so we were warned not to go to the deep end. We also did not know the lagoon had quicksand.

The way to detect quicksand is to notice your foot slowly sinking into the sand. So, as we were swimming, other kids started to scream pretending they were caught in quicksand just to make the others panic.

We decided to swim a bit along the ocean shore. There was this boy who was a very good swimmer. He swam with my Aunty Sarafina on his back and then returned her. I, on the other hand, found it fun and wanted the boy to take me for a swim on his back, too.

I asked the boy, and I thought it was going to be like my Aunty Sarafina's swim ride, but by the time we got to the deep end, the boy just slipped from under me, and before I knew what to do the boy had already got out of the ocean. I went under the water and I didn't know what to do. I was looking under the water for someone or something that I could grab and hold but there was nothing.

The lifeguard just stood there watching me drown, but with Jehovah God watching over me my life was saved by a man who was swimming not far from where I was drowning. He went behind me and slowly pushed me to the ocean shore. I did not drink any ocean water and that also helped stop me from drowning. I said thanks to the man who saved my life. As for the lifeguards who worked at the beach, they stood there and did nothing except for getting mad at the boy for leaving me in the ocean.

Shaking with fear of how I almost lost my life, I told Sarafina, Chakakuka, and Yahgahbo that we should go home. Tamara, after seeing what happened, agreed that we should go home. We left the beach to get a taxi, but it seemed impossible. While waiting for a taxi, a guy drove by in his SUV who was interested in Tamara, so he agreed to give us a ride to her place.

We all got in the SUV and off to Tamara's house we went. When we got to there, we said goodbye, changed our clothes, and went home. After getting home, my grandmother Stuciah asked us how the movie was, and we told her it was great. She then asked which movies we watched, and we gave her names of movies they did not play at the video club. We didn't know that while we were at the beach, my grandmother Stuciah went to the video club and asked for us.

The people who worked at the video club told my grandmother Stuciah that we did not go there, so she knew we had lied and that we went with Tamara to the beach. My grandmother said, "OK, you all come here and let me see if there is sand in your hair and salt on your skin." When my grandmother Stuciah checked our hair, there was beach sand in it, and when she put her tongue on our skin, she tasted salt.

My grandmother Stuciah said to us, "You guys better start explaining where you are coming from." Sarafina didn't want us to say anything, but Yahgahbo said we went to the beach with Tamara and that I almost drowned in the ocean. At that, my grandmother Stuciah said, "You see, I told you guys not to go to the beach without me knowing about it. What if something terrible had happened, what would I have told your mother?"

My grandmother Stuciah said to us, "From now on, I better not hear that you all went to the beach." We promised never to go to the beach again, and if you ask me, I never wanted to go again because I almost lost my life. Because of what happened to me, there was no more going to the beach with Tamara and her friends. We stayed at home and played with the friends we had who lived in the same area.

We needed something to do to keep us busy, so we thought we would talk to my Aunty Peyeeh about opening a business for us. She told us to think about what it was that we wanted to do, and once we figured it out we should go to her and tell her what our business plans were, and then she would give us money for us to start it.

We told Aunty Peyeeh that we would like to start our own orange business, so she told us to give her time to think about it and to also discuss it with my grandmother Stuciah to see if she agreed.

# CHAPTER 10

# THE RETURN OF MY MOTHER: HER SAD STORY

Aunty Peyeeh decided that instead of always giving us money to buy stuff for ourselves, she would buy us bags of oranges so we could start our own orange business. When Aunty Peyeeh bought the bags of oranges for us to sell, Aunty Wawanibo wasn't home; she had gone to visit one of her European boyfriends, so she wasn't around to know what was going on. We got ourselves a table with three dish trays to peel and put the oranges on, and each of us had our own moneybag around our waist to put our money in after people bought from us.

It was fun and exciting to have our own business where we could learn how to make our own money. The selling of the oranges went great, plus there were other kids whose parents allowed them to sell on the streets very late at night. When we would sell the oranges on the street late at night, we would wave down cars and pretend to be going somewhere very far and then the taxi driver would refuse us.

At that time, men in cars with dark windows were kidnapping people, even kids, and we did not care much. We kept doing it, and some taxi drivers who travelled the road often took notice of what we were doing and started agreeing to take us, but then we would refuse and run.

One day while selling oranges, I decided to wave down a private car that went by very fast very late that night, and the car stopped. I noticed the window of the car was very dark, even though they had stopped at a distance, so I decided not to go and pretend I wanted a ride, but to my surprise the car started to reverse to where we all were standing and we all left what we were selling and ran for our lives. We hid somewhere for a while and the car waited for a bit, then drove off to wherever they were going, and we came back to our market, packed up, and left for home.

Each day was the same routine: we would take a bag of oranges and go to the streets to sell them and hang with our friends who sold other stuff. One day while selling oranges on the street, my Aunty Wawanibo came home after a long visit at one of her boyfriend's and she saw that we were on the street very late that night.

She stopped the taxi she was in and got down to ask us what we were doing out on the street so late; we told her that Aunty Peyeeh had bought us bags of oranges and told us to sell them so we could have spending money. Wawanibo got very mad, and said that when she opened her eyes the oranges better be on their way back to the house and we better be in bed, and in the morning she was going to have a serious talk with our grandmother Stuciah for allowing us on the street so late at night.

The next morning, Aunty Wawanibo was still very mad and told our grandmother Stuciah to stop allowing us to be out late at night on the street. My grandmother Stuciah told her that at least Aunty Peyeeh had her own money and bought things to help keep us busy and to bring money to help buy food for the house, and then she said to my Aunty Wawanibo, "What do you do in this house except complain about everything?"

My grandmother Stuciah said to my Aunty Wawanibo that when Wawanibo gets money, she hides it from everyone, and when she buys food it is only for her to eat alone, so she didn't want to hear Wawanibo complain anymore about us selling oranges late at night on the street, because if Wawanibo was helping in the house we wouldn't have to be out there trying to make some money to help out with food and other stuff at home.

Aunty Wawanibo walked away, saying that if anything happened to her sister Deborah's children, my grandmother Stuciah would be held responsible for that because each time she tried to discipline us my grandmother Stuciah would try and stop her. After that, my Aunty Wawanibo made it her business to come to the road where we sold our oranges every night just before midnight to tell us to pack up and go home, because she was going to allow us to be up late selling oranges, but not after midnight.

We packed up and left to go home, and once we got there we talked about everything that went on while we sold. We talked about who had a crush on whom, we talked about who was now having sex at a very early age, we talked about whose parents were strict on them and whose parents allowed them to be free to do whatever they wanted. When we went to the road to sell the oranges, there would be boys who would come around for a visit, some in our own age group and some a few years older. There was one person who I used to like very much. His name was Momo and he had a brother name Jolo.

One day when Jolo came around, I asked him if he could tell his brother that I liked him, but at that time my hair was cut very short, almost bald, because I had lice in it and my grandmother Stuciah had cut it very short so she could get rid of the lice from my hair.

When his brother Momo asked him who the girl was that was interested in him, Jolo told him he would bring him to meet me. That evening when he brought his brother to meet me, I saw them from afar because I was on the road selling oranges. I was very nervous about what I would say to this boy, because he was a bit older and I had not shown any interest until then, because almost all my little friends had boyfriends.

When they got to where I was standing with other friends, Momo asked his brother where the girl was, and his brother replied, saying, "Here, here's the boy." I wanted the ground to open up and swallow me, because I was so ashamed that his brother called me a boy because my hair was cut short. Momo told his brother, "Why didn't you tell me it was a boy?" and they laughed and said nothing to me; he just kept walking, and after he walked for a short distance, they stopped, turned back, and kept laughing as they walked away.

Each time after that, whenever he and his brother walked by I would run and hide, or sometimes I would pretend not to notice them at all. We started to attend meetings regularly at the Kingdom Hall of Jehovah's Witnesses, and that helped me to understand more about the difference between the right thing and the wrong thing. I fell in love with knowing more about Jehovah God and his son Jesus Christ and those who were blessed to be the friends of Jehovah God, and I learned what happens to people who learn about Jehovah God but refuse to serve him.

I noticed that once I started to get close to Jehovah God, my Aunty Sarafina wouldn't hang out with me anymore. She made new friends, and sometimes when I went to meetings at the Kingdom Hall of Jehovah's Witnesses, she wouldn't come with me, and even when she went with me she would just sleep through the meeting.

I started attending meetings regularly and had my Bible studies on the weekend. I know the things I was learning were the truth because of realizations later on in my life.

One day while at home, my Aunty Wawanibo came running in, saying, "Deborah's here!" All my uncles came running to greet her and I just could not believe that I was seeing my mother. I did not know what else to do, I just ran to her, gave her a big hug, and started crying. I did not want to let go of her for fear I would never see her again.

Yahgahbo came running and crying, too, but Chakakuka was out playing with his friends. When he returned, we told him Mama was home; he said we were lying and trying to pull his leg, so we told him to go inside and see for himself. He started to believe a little when he saw us with new things. My grandmother Stuciah's house was overcrowded with people who came to greet my mother, and some of them knew my mother when she was a baby and others only knew her by hearing my grandmother Stuciah speak of her whenever they asked whose kids we were.

When my mother saw my brother, she started crying because she had never been away from her kids for this long before. That night, no one in the house slept; we all sat up late listening to the sad story of all my mother endured just to get back to us. She told us that the man who we knew to be our stepdad Mr. AmiShasi did not treat her so well. She said that when we were in Ivory Coast, he wanted her to let Aunty Umo send us to Nigeria, and when she refused his mistreatment started.

He locked her up in his five-story building house with a big yard and a fence that was taller than the house. She was not allowed to leave the house on her own unless the driver took her out shopping, or the brothers and sisters picked her up to attend meetings at the Kingdom Hall of Jehovah's Witnesses.

My mother said Mr. AmiShasi had a special room in the house that only he had the key to, and she was strongly warned never to open that door. She said sometimes she would wonder what was in there. She told us that sometimes when she would sleep during the day, her body would get heavy and her mouth would become mute and she would be unable to scream for help.

She said that one day she woke up and opened her eyes and her body refused to move, and she saw a strange person coming toward her, and she tried to scream but her voice wouldn't come out no matter how much she tried. As the person got closer, she felt death itself, and the only thing she remembered doing was slowly calling Jehovah's name in her heart and mind, and slowly she untangled herself from whatever held her captive. As that happened, she found herself screaming the name Jehovah God out loud when she was set free.

The maid that worked for them came running to her room to find out if she was OK, and when she explained what happened the maid warned her to be very careful because most Nigerian men have a special place in their home called the Shrine, where they practiced voodoo, and because of that the house they live in can be possessed by an evil spirit.

The woman told her to keep praying, and that if she had a church she needed to go there all the time to stay safe. My mother said that Mr. AmiShasi threatened her, saying that if she didn't allow us to go to Nigeria she would never see us again; he also told her that from then on she was not allowed to leave the house to go to the market or to attend meetings at the Kingdom Hall of Jehovah's Witnesses. After not seeing her at the Kingdom Hall for many weeks, the brothers and sisters came to where they lived to check up on her and to plead with Mr. AmiShasi to allow her to go and worship, but he refused and asked them to leave.

She said he would come home very late at night or not come home at all, and if she questioned him, he would beat her up badly. She said what kept her strong was that she would read her Bible and try to stay close to Jehovah God. She said she would sometimes give the security guard money so she could go out and buy foodstuffs and other things that she could bring with her back to Liberia. She said after she bought those things, she gave them to the sisters at the Kingdom Hall of Jehovah's Witnesses to keep for her.

My mother said that she wanted to know what was in the room Mr. AmiShasi kept a special key for, so one day she stole the key when he was on his way out, and she waited for about an hour and then finally decided that she was going to open the door. She said that as she walked to the door, her feet started to get heavy and her whole body felt different. When she finally opened the door, she said something called her into the room and she could not control herself.

In the middle of the room was a giant African cooking pot, and a woman was walking around the pot, stirring it, saying nothing. She said there was a snake in the pot and the woman just kept stirring. There were all kinds of voodoo stuff in the room. She wasn't sure what happened next, because she passed out before anything else could happen.

My mother said it was Mr. AmiShasi who picked her up and took her to her room, because when she woke up she found herself lying in their bed, and he told her that she was very lucky to be alive and that she should never, ever enter that room again. My mother said she planned her escape from Mr. AmiShasi for many months, and it was one of his cousins that helped connect her to a captain of one of the big ships that was scheduled to leave for Liberia.

When it was time for her to leave, she told him that she would like to attend a meeting at the Kingdom Hall, and he told her that it was OK for her to go but she should make sure to return right after. She said it was as if he could sense that she would not return. She said her life with him was like the movie *Sleeping with the Enemy.* That evening, she attended a meeting at the Kingdom Hall, and then the brothers and sisters gave her a ride to the harbour where the ship was. When she arrived, they helped her unpack all her things onto the ship, and told her to have a safe trip and to contact them when she arrived in Liberia.

She knew it would not be long before Mr. AmiShasi started to look for her, so the captain of the ship told her to hide in the engine room until the ship left Nigeria. She said she stayed down in the engine room for a week, and the next thing she knew, Mr. AmiShasi brought the entire army on board the ship to search for her. She said she could hear all the noise they were making in their search for her, and her life depended on staying mute and not making a sound.

She said Mr. AmiShasi and the army checked everywhere on the ship, and then they got to the engine room and Mr. AmiShasi insisted he wanted to check it as well, but the captain told him no. He said to Mr. AmiShasi that he had allowed him to check his ship but would not allow him into the engine room. She said Mr. AmiShasi knew she was in there, but he had no right to check, so he left. After being on the sea for a very long time, the ship finally made it to Liberia, and oh, how happy she was just to see us again.

I was also very happy to see her, as were my brother and sister. To know that she was now safe was very satisfying to me. We all finally fell asleep, but were all up very early the next morning from excitement.

My mother brought us so many things with the help of the brothers and sisters at the Kingdom Hall of Jehovah's Witnesses, including food. Things between my mother and her sisters were fine for a bit, but when the little money my mother had was gone, things became different. They weren't all that kind anymore, and they started to tell my mother, "When you were living life here in Liberia with Mr. AmiShasi, you were up and thought you wouldn't come down."

They would get into fights with my mother, and because I was too young to defend her, I would bite whoever my mother was in a fight with, either my grandmother Stuciah, Aunty Wawanibo, or Peyeeh, and I would hear them say, "You see, your daughter just bit me, and if she bites me again you will see what I will do to her." Sometimes I would go out somewhere alone and just cry and wish things would get better for us. I would sometimes say to myself, "I bet if we had a father, none of this would happen to us."

Because of what my mother went through with her family, she always kept her kids close to Jehovah God, because she always believed in him and that he makes things possible for us, and he does. As we attended meetings regularly at the Kingdom Hall, I soon became an unbaptized publisher, and started preaching to people about Jehovah's ways and His purpose for humankind and His promise of a good life and a happy family. I was soon teaching the Bible to many people and telling them how to live right with Jehovah God. It brought comfort to me just knowing that all of this pain and suffering would not last for long.

When Chakakuka and Uncle Dudu saw how serious I was about serving Jehovah God, they were soon baptized and started preaching full-time. It was not long until my mother found a place for us to live behind City Hall in an apartment building.

It was a two-bedroom apartment building; my mother had her own room, and I shared a room with Chakakuka and Yahgahbo. My mother told me that I was the new mother in the house, because most times she would not be around to do stuff for us, such as cooking, cleaning, and helping us with our homework, because she had to work two jobs to take care of us.

She said it would be my responsibility to make sure everything got done right in the house, and that if I needed any help, I should ask Chakakuka and Yahgahbo to help me. If they refused to help, when she returned I should let her know and she would discipline them. My mother worked two jobs: one was a manager at a hotel during the day and the other was a manager for a night club.

I know as you read this you are saying, "Damn, how could she care for three kids?" Well, we were well-disciplined kids who followed instructions. We were told that we were allowed to go play with our friends once all the work in the house was done. At 6:00 p.m., we would get water and put it in the apartment for uses like flushing the toilet, bathing, and cooking; at 7:00 p.m., we would shower; and before 8:00 p.m., our school homework would be completed; and by 9:00 p.m. we were in bed for school the next day. My mother made sure she came home every night after work and on the weekends.

My mother had a special whistle that she would blow when she got home at night. I would run down the stairs to open the main entrance door to the apartment building for her. Sometimes Chakakuka and I would sit up all night waiting for her to come home, but when it was a school day, my mother hated for us to wait up late because she didn't want us to not have enough sleep and wake up late for school. But even with that I still waited up for her, because I wanted to make sure she got home safe. Taking the responsibilities of the next mother in the house was not easy for a young girl. When we got home after school, I would put down my backpack and quickly pick up the list of what food my mother wanted me to cook, and I would run to the market to buy these things and then come home to cook. Chakakuka and Yahgahbo were supposed to help me around the house with things like cleaning and dirty dishes, but they would leave all of it for me to do and they would go and play.

It hurt me, because I felt like the stepchild and I did not have a chance to play and be a kid, because I was too busy being a mother to my brother and sister. Most times, I would just watch them play from upstairs while I multitasked with the house cleaning, cooking, and doing the dishes. Then, when the food was ready, I would call them to come and eat, and it took them no time to be up the stairs to eat, but when I asked them to help me, they would never show up.

Whenever my mother got home and I tried to tell her about this, she would not do anything about it, because she had been busy all day and was tired, so I started to think as a mother and asked myself what a mother would do if her kids did not follow her instructions. The answer came to me: she would punish them. So, I decided that if I asked them for help and they refused, when I was done cooking I would give them very little to eat, and then next time when I asked them they would help me around the house.

I had a friend name Shas, who used to live upstairs, who went through the same thing as me, so I told her about my plan to make my brother and sister help me around the house. She also agreed to do the same, so we decided we would take our parents' food out first and then eat together before we called them for their food, so that way, even if they complained about the food not being enough, there would be no more food left to give them.

The first time I ever tried that discipline method, I was afraid that Chakakuka, who was the oldest, would get mad and beat me up for not giving him enough food to eat, but though the fear was there about how they would react, I still had to do it because that was the only way I could get them to help me. When it was time for them to eat, they came home running, thinking I had given them all the food that I cooked, but to their surprise the food I gave them wasn't enough to keep them full until the next day.

Chakakuka got very mad, and said that when our mother got home he was going to make a report about my actions, and Yahgahbo said that she was not going to eat her food until our mother got home from work.

Considering the fact that my mother got home very late from work most times, I wasn't sure if Yahgahbo could wait that long before she ate the food that was given to her. Well, like she said, she waited and waited, but my mother didn't return, so Yahgahbo got very hungry, ate her food, and promised to tell my mother the next day.

As for me, I really did not care, because I knew I made the right decision, and very soon they would know how important it was for them to help me. The next day, when they told our mother what I did to them, she said, "Well, I told you guys that when I am not around Arnelle is the next mother in the house, so if you are not helping her do any work around the house, she has the right to decide what to do, and if you dare disobey her you won't find it very funny when I get back."

After that day, things around the house started to get better. I could finally get them to help me get things done around the house, and when the jobs were done early, I, too, got the chance to go out and play with my friends. It was hard for me, because I had to be the one always yelling and telling them what needed to be done.

Most times, there would be only a little water left in the water barrel, just enough for me to cook food. It hurts that I was left with such a huge responsibility to care for my older brother and my younger sister as a mother, when I did not even know what being a mother meant, but I guess every woman is born with the inborn tendency to be a mother, and that was how I survived being a mother to them.

I also had to make sure we did our own Bible study for meetings at the Kingdom Hall of Jehovah's Witnesses. Most times, we would even attend meetings by ourselves by walking there, and when asked by the brothers and sisters where our mother was, we would tell them she was busy at work, but sometimes she would come with us on Sundays.

The days my mother stayed home, she would make sure that everything around the house was spotless and she herself would cook. When she did, she would make a very big meal, because she was expecting her friends to come over. My mother had many male friends, because she claimed females were always jealous of her and would talk bad about her behind her back.

Being that young, I never clearly got all that my mother was going through, but I kind of understood a little from the sad music she played that told me she was missing someone, or from the way she would lock her bedroom door and silently cry. Most times I would go to her door and just listen, and I wanted to just give her a hug and tell her everything was going to be OK, but this was a woman who would want nothing to worry us and she would act all strong and well put-together.

But deep down inside she was breaking up really badly, and that was breaking me up, too, because each time she would cry, I, too, would silently cry for her, wishing I could save her from whatever it was that was hurting her badly. Chakakuka and Yahgahbo never really paid much attention, because they were too busy out playing with their friends.

One early weekend morning, my mother came home and told us that she was not feeling well and that she would like it if we kept quiet, and she sent my brother and sister out to go and play and asked me if I could make her coffee or Lipton tea. I agreed and quickly ran to the kitchen to make the tea for her. After not too long, I brought the tea to her in her bedroom, but she was too sick to get up so I supported her head and fed her the tea.

She had a high fever, and the next thing I knew she started to vomit, so I ran for a bucket with water in it and a towel to wipe the vomit up. After I cleaned the place up, I begged her to put strength in herself and allow me to help her to the washroom where she could take a bath, because she smelled of vomit. She was able to put strength in herself, and I helped her to the washroom. I put lots of warm water in the tub and gave her a bath, dried her up, and asked her to sit on the lid of the toilet while I ran to her bedroom to change her bedsheets and pillow cases.

Then I helped her to her room, rubbed her down with Vicks rub, and gave her clean clothes to put on. When she was settled in bed, I brought her a cold towel and put it on her forehead to help bring her temperature down. By the early afternoon, she had started to feel a bit better, but she sent Chakakuka to go to the clinic, ask for Doctor Garzax, and tell him to please come because she was not feeling very well.

My brother and sister were very worried when they saw that it was serious. Dr. Garzax came with his doctor's bag, immediately hung an IV on my mother, and gave her some medication, and told us that he would be back to check on her. After he left, Chakakuka, Yahgahbo, and I went into our room and held each other and started crying.

We were scared; we did not want anything bad to happen to her because she was the only parent we had. I then heard my mother call my name. I rushed into the room, and she told me she was going to be OK, that it was just a little fever and Doctor Garzax was taking care of it. She asked me to call Chakakuka and Yahgahbo into the room so she could talk to them as well. When they went in, she told them the same thing, and we held each other and started crying, but she kept telling us not to.

We took the songbook we used for meetings at the Kingdom Hall and started to sing the songs we learned that made her happy. She knew we might be hungry, so she told me to bring her handbag and she gave us some money to go and buy whatever we wanted to eat, and then she asked me to cook something for her. I quickly rushed to the market and bought ingredients to make her a traditional soup that people in my country make when one is not feeling well or has a fever.

It is called pepper soup, and people usually eat it with fufu or rice, and that day I made fufu for her to eat along with it. Chakakuka and Yahgahbo were so well behaved around the house; they made sure it was clean and didn't make any noise. After a few days, my mother was well again and back to being busy working to take care of us, and I was back to being the mother of the house.

One day, I cooked a special traditional soup called palaver sauce with rice, and that day my mother brought home some guests, so I served them and they ate. While eating, they asked my mother who cooked the food; she told them it was me, and they said, "Wow, such a small baby is able to cook like this! That is unbelievable."

They found it hard to believe her, because they said there were much older women who did not know how to cook at all, and they complimented my mother for teaching me such an important household skill. She also told them that I was able to clean the house and go to the market to buy food as well, and bring back change and buy exactly what was asked of me to buy.

As usual, my mother was busy either hanging out with friends or busy at work. I went ahead with my busy life as well, going to school and coming home to be a mother to Chakakuka and Yahgahbo. There was a place called the hand pump, where we used to go to help my brother fetch water. There were many houses around the hand pump, and every kid from around the neighbourhood would go there to fetch water for their parents' home. The hand pump closed at about 6:30 p.m. and was sealed with a lock, so if you didn't get there on time to fetch your water, the lineup got very long.

Most times, there were fights over who would be able to fetch water next or who was there first or who cut the line and cheated. One day, Chakakuka went in late to fetch water, and I am not sure exactly what happened because I wasn't there, but according to him he was ahead of a girl whose family lived across from the hand pump.

The girl claimed Chakakuka wasn't ahead of her, and they started an argument. A friend of mine who was at the hand pump came running to tell me that Chakakuka was having trouble. I went running, and the next thing I knew her older brother was there. He didn't ask any questions, he just tried to jump my brother for a fight, and the girl took our water container and threw it away, so both of us got into a fight, and someone called her other sister and it was like a mini war at the hand pump.

People came and separated us, and the guy who oversaw the hand pump came and said to us that there was no need for what was going on, and even though it was time for him to close the pump, he would allow us both to fetch water for our family. He said that the next time it happened he would stop us from getting water there for a few days. That hand pump was the only one in that area, and we didn't have a wheelbarrow to go elsewhere for the water we needed for taking showers, flushing, etc.

I told Chakakuka that if he did not want me telling our mother what happened at the hand pump, he'd better make sure he was there very early to fetch the water for the house and be gone from there before the rush and all the drama started. He agreed, and from then on water was in our house on time and he had enough time to go out and play with his friends. Yahgahbo made sure she washed all the dirty dishes before I was done cooking and swept the entire house, and then went out to play with her friends.

When all that was done, the food was on time, they had enough to eat, and everyone was happy. When all of my work was done, I would sometimes go downstairs and play with them and our other friends. There was this friend by the name of Regnah; she was very wild and would run around with all the boys. She was a tomboy, so one day while out playing with her, she took us into this bush.

She said she knew what made girls have big breasts. We said "Really?" She said yes, so we all followed her, and she took a certain leaf and said when you put the liquid from the leaf on your nipples your breasts would start to grow. We put the liquid of the leaf on our chests, but no breasts grew there, so for the next few days she told us there was a certain bug that when it bites your nipples your breasts would grow. We all looked for that special bug to bite our nipples. She found this bug and put it on her nipple; it bit her and she screamed. When it was our turn to try it, we all refused and started running away.

Shas's parents and my mother knew each other very well, and sometimes when we were both done our housework we would go into her room and she would claim to know how to read cards, because she saw her stepmother do it.

She would read my cards, and sometimes my brother's and sister's cards as well. She would talk about people who were interested in us, but we just did it for fun because none of it meant anything to us, we were all much too young to pay attention to who was interested in us. Most times when we had nothing to do, we would all sit and tell each other stories we had been told by others. Shas attended the same Mounsorado International School as us, and most times we would go to school and return home together so we were all safe.

Chakakuka is mixed with Liberian and Lebanese because his father is Lebanese. Chakakuka's father's brother's name is Tommy, and he owns a business and didn't live far from where we stayed. Chakakuka's Uncle Tommy told my mother that he would pay for us to get a tutor who would help us with our schoolwork at his house. The first time we visited for our tutoring, we saw that our brother's Uncle Tommy had a cat almost as big as a dog.

Tommy's cat got to eat a whole chicken prepared by his chef, and for me that was a "wow," because people were hungry and dying because of lack of food, and this guy's cat gets to eat a whole chicken. The tutor came to teach us, but most times we were too busy paying attention to how many girls came in and out of Uncle Tommy's house. People started to warn my mother that it was not a good idea to let us go over to the house to study, because we got to see all kinds of things, like young girls smoking and drinking alcohol.

Therefore, my mother told Uncle Tommy that she would prefer it if the teacher came over to where we lived and helped us with our homework. He agreed, and the tutor started teaching us at our house. Things started to fall into place, and our lives were OK. We were getting to love our new environment and made many new friends.

One day, our neighbour's cat had kittens and they gave me one. When I brought it home, Chakakuka and Yahgahbo were very happy, so we used the little money that was left from buying food to buy milk for the kitten. The kitten was very playful, and we found it so much fun, but when our mother came home and found we had a kitten in the house she said we needed to give it back to the owner, because cats are related to witchcraft and she did not want any of that in her apartment.

We begged and begged, but none of it helped, so I had to return the kitten to its owner. We were very sad about that because we had nothing to play with. It wasn't long before I learned that one of our neighbour's dogs was pregnant and would soon be having her puppies, so I went over and made a request to please have one of the puppies when her dog gave birth, and she agreed. Oh, I just could not wait.

Her dog was due in just a few weeks and I was excited. When I finally got my puppy—my very first puppy and the only one I ever had—I brought him home and Chakakuka and Yahgahbo just fell in love with him, and we weren't sure what our mom would think so we waited for her to get home before we got too excited about it. To our surprise, when our mother saw how beautiful and chubby he was, she immediately fell in love with him. She said she would need to scrub him down before allowing him in the house to stay, just in case he had anything contagious, because she didn't want him making us sick.

She put lukewarm water with some shampoo in the tub we washed our clothes in and scrubbed him good. He didn't like it at first, but when he figured out that it was for his own good, he accepted it. My mother started to fall in love with him and sent us to get milk for him to drink; she also took her time training him where to poop and pee, when to take a nap, and when to eat.

He started getting big and was very playful. We had so much fun watching him grow, and then one day there was a knock on the door. When we opened it, it was an old person who looked identical to my mother. Something told me they were related, and my guess was right. He told us he was the father to our mother, so we let him in, gave him something to eat, and took his bags into our bedroom.

My mother wasn't home, so we sat up with him until her return, and while we were waiting, he told us stories about when he was growing up and how he met our grandmother. He was twenty and my grandmother was fourteen when she got pregnant, and fifteen when they had my mother. My grandmother felt her childhood was taken away from her and that she needed to party. She would leave my mother home alone locked in a room with candles left on when she was a baby.

My grandmother Stuciah would go out to party with friends and come home very late. My grandfather, whose name was Borlor, said that when he would ask my grandmother why she would leave the baby alone in the room crying and go out with friends to have fun, she would tell him she didn't care and it was none of his business. He said he would get very mad knowing my mother was left home alone as a baby; the two of them would get into a fight.

My grandfather Borlor said my grandmother Stuciah decided not to live with him anymore, because she said he was way older than her and she wanted to enjoy her life. She told him that he was too controlling, and she wanted to live freely. My grandfather Borlor said that he asked that my mother Deborah be given to him so he could take better care of her, but my grandmother Stuciah refused to give him the baby and he had to move out.

My grandmother Stuciah wouldn't allow him to see or spend time with his daughter and that's why he moved elsewhere in the country. My grandmother Stuciah went on with her life, and he made a family of his own. My grandfather Borlor also contracted leprosy when he was away and it ate up all his fingers and toes, but what amazed me was that he could still construct bags, hats, fans, mats, and other stuff with his hand that had no fingers.

My grandfather Borlor promised to teach me how to construct things as well. We just could not wait for my mother to get home to find her surprise, but we were surprised when she got home. She was more upset than surprised, because she said he abandoned her and took care of his wife and other kids and left her to suffer with her mother. She said that when she was in her teens and she ran away from her mother to go live with him, her stepmother didn't want her at their house and her father asked her to leave.

That night was a very sad night, because my mother was crying and my grandfather Borlor was crying too, begging my mother to forgive him. My mother said that the only reason he came was because he was old and now needed her to take care of him. He said to her that was not the reason he came. He said he came because he needed her forgiveness for not being there for her when she needed him.

The next morning, they talked and talked and my grandfather told my mother that he would like to make up for the lost time between them by staying and taking care of us, and taking us to attend meetings at the Kingdom Hall of Jehovah's Witnesses while she was at work, but my mother was very concerned about his leprosy because she heard it was contagious and she didn't want us get infected by it. He reassured her that he was cured of it and that there was nothing to worry about.

My mother agreed, and said she would see how things worked out, but my grandfather staying over didn't last long because when my mother told her mother Stuciah that her father Borlor had come to find her and was staying over at her place, my grandmother Stuciah didn't like that at all. My grandmother Stuciah got very mad, and said that he wanted to claim a child he did not work for after he had abandoned my mother for so long.

She said all kinds of horrible things to my mother about her father, and it made my mother even angrier instead of more forgiving, and when my mother told my grandmother Stuciah that her dad also had leprosy which took away all his fingers, it made matters worse. My grandmother Stuciah said that it was the wickedness of my grandfather Borlor that caught up with him, and that my mother should get him out of our house as soon as possible before we all got leprosy.

My grandfather Borlor started teaching us how to make bags and hats from just straws, and in the evening he would help us with our schoolwork and we would do our Bible study together.

One day, my mother came home and said she wanted to have a word with our grandfather Borlor, so she sent us into the room. I was hoping it was some good news, like he would be staying forever, but I guess I was wrong. I heard her crying and I knew it was not good, and I heard him cry as well because he was about to leave his grandchildren, and he would not get the chance to know us.

My mother came into the room to explain why it was important that our grandfather Borlor left, and her only excuse was that he had leprosy and she didn't want to make us sick. I interrupted her and told her that he said it was cured, but she replied saying she can't trust it. Our grandfather Borlor came in after she left our room and gave us hugs and said he was going to miss us greatly. We could not stop crying.

We helped him pack his bags and watched him leave, and I was really hurt and kept wondering why she couldn't forgive him. But the truth is she did forgive him, but after she talked to our grandmother Stuciah, she brought back the pain my mother was trying to let go of and seeing her father Borlor around was going to remind her of it and she just couldn't take it. After her father Borlor left she was sad for days, and when Chakakuka and Yahgahbo were out playing I would hear her cry alone in her room.

My mother had truly been hurt by everyone she trusted, but being so young there were things she couldn't talk about to us that she kept deep inside, but her tears made me understand the depth of her pain. After our grandfather Borlor left, my mother brought in Debe to watch over us. We called Debe our aunty because we had been used to her since we were kids. Debe is the ex-girlfriend of my Uncle Sokoka, and she needed a place to stay because she and her older sister were having a problem and my mother needed someone to watch us while she was not home.

The time came when Chakakuka was to be circumcised. My mother did not know that the doctor she chose had never done circumcisions before and that Chakakuka was his first patient. I'm not sure what the doctor did, but he claims he put my brother to sleep. Whatever he did wore off and my brother was not asleep anymore, and he could feel every pain that was brought upon him. As we sat outside, I could hear him yell and scream at the top of his lungs.

He was screaming that my mother Deborah should get him out of there, and that the doctor and those who worked with him were wicked and angels of the devil. The things he said and the way in which he said them were funny and sad at the same time. When everything was over, my mother thought the doctor did a good job, so she brought my brother home. He was not allowed to wear pants, so he put a wrap around himself and waited for his penis to heal, but instead of healing it started to swell and got infected.

My mother contacted Doctor Garzax, who had experience with circumcision, and when he came over and examined my brother's penis, he said my mother should count herself lucky that she called him just in time, because my brother's penis might have become rotten.

He said Chakakuka would have lost his manhood as a little boy if he wasn't treated on time. So, Doctor Garzax had to do another surgery on my brother, and I felt sorry for him because of the pain he had to endure. Everything went well and my brother started healing properly. When my mother saw that Doctor Garzax was good, she went and got my Aunty Wawanibo's son Tukar so he could get his done, but she didn't tell him that was the reason for bringing him.

All Tukar knew was that he was coming to spend some time with us for a bit and would later return home. When Tukar arrived and saw that my brother was circumcised and he wasn't wearing pants, Tukar started to laugh and tease him, until one day my brother said to him, "Don't worry, soon it will be your turn, too." It was not long before my mother sent for Doctor Garzax to come over and circumcise Tukar.

Tukar thought it was all a joke at first, until Doctor Garzax gave him something for the pain, laid him on the table in our living room, and told us to hold him. Doctor Garzax began his circumcision process. It was nasty to watch, and I still cannot believe we survived seeing that; but hey, we did and he is still alive. When Doctor Garzax was all done, Tukar said he hated him and never wanted to see him again.

My mother allowed Tukar to stay a bit so he could heal, but each time we wanted to scare him or make him cry when he was misbehaving, we just told him Doctor Garzax was coming and he would start to cry or get really scared and behave himself. When it was time for Tukar to return home, we were sad because he would not be there to play with us. It was not long after Tukar left that our family friend Debe left, too, and that made us sad, because we had gotten used to them being around. We carried on with our usual day-to-day, though we felt alone not having anyone else around.

Just when we thought life was starting to get back to normal, we woke up to the sound of gunfire and people running up and down in confusion. All thanks to Jehovah God that my mother was home that morning and told us to lie flat on the ground and not to move until she found out what was happening, but as soon as she went downstairs, we poked our head over the balcony to find out what was going on. Just then a stray bullet hit someone who was walking by my mother, and people started running.

My mother came back and told us to stay low, but to also try to pack some things that were important to us that we could take with us, and that we should not open the door for anyone. She said she was going to go out there and find a way for us to escape to safety. There was a long-time friend of our stepfather's called Doctor Alevf who helped my mother get us a visa to go to Nigeria. My mother got the visa for us to go from Liberia to Nigeria, and she returned with some foodstuffs and other emergency items that we would need for our trip on the ECOMOG (Economic Community of West African States Monitoring Group) gunship.

The ship was to leave in a week to Nigeria, so in the meantime my mother got herself ready by preparing things we would need at sea. She made stuff like pepper with vinegar in jars, deep-fried dried chicken, and meat and fried pepper sauce. She packed what we called Gari—it's made of grated and dried cassava—some bread, water to drink, fruit juice tanks, Nido milk, and lots of other stuff I can't really remember. My mother made sure she packed everything that we would need, including clothes, underclothes, bodywash, shampoo & conditioner, toothpaste, toothbrushes, and first-aid items. My mother has always been a true survivor; I'm not sure how she did it, but she did and she kept us safe. It was time to leave everything behind once more, including our friends and our puppy.

# Chapter 11

# The April 6, 1996 War: Our Escape to Nigeria and Then Ghana

I'm not sure what happened to our puppy after being left alone with no one to look after him. There was no taking our puppy with us on the ECOMOG gunboat, because no dogs or other animals were allowed, plus people were more concerned about saving their own lives than worrying about their pets. In our case, we had no choice but to leave our puppy behind. We were woken up very early in the morning by our stepfather's very close friend Dr. Alevf with a car that was arranged to pick us up and take us all the way to the port to where the ships were.

The place is called Freeport, and that is where we would wait to board the Nigerian gunboat. My mother made sure we were dressed up properly to board the ship, because she said it got cold on the ocean. The car waited for us downstairs and our things were packed into it. Most of our neighbours were still in their apartments, not knowing where they would go next.

We heard that the April 6 war was going to be one of the worst wars Liberia had ever had, with lots of bloodshed, and my mother didn't want us to be a part of it. We said goodbye to our neighbours with tears in our eyes, for we did not know if we would ever see each other again, or if they would even be alive after everything.

As the car drove away, we could not stop waving goodbye. On our way to Freeport, I saw people in a panic with their clothes and other stuff wrapped in bundles on their heads going to wherever their feet could take them, all in the name of safety. On our way, there was a lot of traffic because too many people were trying to head to safety. There was a huge line of people, from young ones to old ones, all trying to head to find a relative who lived where they could be safe, but nowhere was ever safe because no one was allowed to leave the country.

There was a saying that the 1996 war was called No Way Out—it was going to be very bloody and a lot of people wouldn't even make it out alive. As we were getting closer to Freeport, there was a huge line-up of people trying to get inside for safety, and they even threatened that they were going to close the gate to the port because it was getting overcrowded, but with my mother's big connections at the port she was able to get some people in.

We finally got in, and shortly afterward the gate to the port was closed and no one else was allowed to come in. I was surprised at the number of people who were waiting in line just to get on the gunboat. Some people had slept there for days just trying to get their families out, but luckily for us our stepfather had close connections with the Nigerian ambassador, so the ambassador wrote a letter for my mother to give to the captain of the boat when she went to get us our visa, and that letter made us VIPs, meaning we were first in line to get on the boat.

I was amazed how huge these ships were. They were so tall you had to almost look up to the sky to see their tops. I had never seen something so huge and great before in my life.

The ships were beautiful, and I called them the queens of the sea, because the sea guides them to wherever they wanted to go, and he knows that they would never leave him. When it came time for us to board the boat, my mother handed the letter along with our passport with the Nigerian visa in it to the captain. He spoke in his language to some of the boys that worked for him and they came to help us with our luggage and put us somewhere safe on the boat.

It was not a special room; it was outside among other people on the ground, but it was an OK spot where we could be a bit comforted. But the fun and scary part was when it was time for us to get on the boat. We had to walk across on a flat walkway with no handles, and I almost passed out. One of the navy guys helped me and told me to not look down, to hold on tight to his hand, and not to let go. As we walked across, I could not help but cry because I was very much afraid and did not want to fall into the water.

One of the guys put Yahgahbo on his back. Chakakuka was just a bit scared, but very excited that he was going to be on a boat on top of the ocean. Another person helped my mother to cross because she was a bit afraid. We got settled in and the boat was scheduled to leave the next day in the morning, but my mother had made sure she had brought enough blankets for us to lay on.

We were so tired that we went to bed without any trouble. When it was morning, my mother had a little bucket for us to spit in after we brushed our teeth, then she would throw it away where people were assigned to shower. It was a place at the end of the boat that met with the ocean, but water never got in, only out, so people were allowed to shower and take a pee there.

It was never for anyone to take a shit, there was a place for that, and then it got sent into the ocean. Most times, there would be a line-up for it, so my mother found the time when it wouldn't be busy and she would take us to shit, and after she would give us water to wash our butts and then she would go between the ship and the ocean and dump the shit into the ocean, sanitize the bucket, and put it away until next time.

Sometimes at night when everyone was sleeping and we needed to pee-pee, my mother would take us so we could go with a flashlight, and we made sure not to step on anyone sleeping on the floor. We would go to the back of the ship; she would give us a little bucket to pee-pee in, and then she would throw it into the ocean and we would go back to sleeping on the floor. We were on the ocean for three days when water started to enter the gunboat, so the captain had to turn the ship around and go back to Freeport in Liberia to find out what was wrong.

For three days we were on that gunboat, scared for our lives as water kept coming into the boat. When we finally made it to Freeport, we were all glad to be alive and safely arrived. Before everyone left the gunboat so it could be checked, the captain asked that everyone put their names down on the paper he was sending out, so that when the boat was fixed he could call the names of those on the list and they were the only people allowed back on.

When we all got down from the gunboat, there were many other people waiting at the port for boats to take them out of Liberia, but there was no boat available to take them, so when they saw our boat they hoped that there might be space for them to leave the country. My mother told us to stay very close to her so that we did not go missing.

My mother advised us to always stay close to the boat so that we would not miss our chance to leave. We all slept outside on the ground in the open cold air, but it was a lot better than losing our chance to leave to safety. After the boat was fixed, the captain started to call names and we were not far from being first in line. We got on the boat and settled in a much better spot than our original one.

Once everyone who was originally on the boat was settled and it was time for the boat to leave, some people tried to jump onto the boat but fell in the water. Some died and others were taken out of the water. The captain could not take more people for fear that the boat would sink, so we continued with our journey to Nigeria. While on the gunboat, Chakakuka and I made friends with one of the navy men who took such a liking to me.

He would allow us to go to his cabin and even allowed us on deck, which no one was allowed to do, and that made me feel special. The navy person whose name I cannot remember would bring food and things that we needed to my mother for us, but my mother still warned us to be very careful. One day, while Chakakuka and I were up on deck watching the ocean, we saw dolphins swimming, and it was an amazing view to behold. After a few days of being on the ocean, we finally arrived in Nigeria at the port in Lagos.

It felt really good to be safe and alive, and though it was fun being on the ocean, we were glad to finally be on land. There were many sick people leaving the boat as well. I'm not sure how they were going to make it, but I guess somehow they did, and though we weren't going to see one another again my hope was that they were OK.

# CHAPTER 12

# FINALLY IN NIGERIA

The feeling of finally being safe was so good, and we just could not wait to get off the ship and onto the land once again. My mother went ahead to make sure we didn't lose any luggage when they unloaded the ship, but the captain promised her that they would look after her luggage with care. Everyone was asked to line-up so that we could exit the ship, which we all did, but by the time we landed on the ground we were unable to walk properly because we had gotten so used to the way we walked on the ocean.

People at the Nigerian port were happy to greet us, and some of them started to ask where we had come from, and then there was this unknown guy who came to me and out of kindness offered me money. My mother told us not to accept anything from a stranger, so I refused to accept the guy's money, but my mother accepted it instead and said thank you. We collected our bags and my mother told us that we would stay for a bit at our stepfather's friend's place, which she had the address of.

When we finally arrived, the person had left for work and would not be coming home anytime soon, but we met his wife and kids and they embraced us into their home, and even gave us a room to stay in. I noticed the wife wasn't too happy that she was unaware of our arrival, but her older kids convinced her to let us stay, because my mother told them that their father was a friend of our stepfather's, and the purpose of our coming to Nigeria was to search for him because we lost contact, but there's more to the story than what was told and we would find that out later.

We were given one bedroom to share with my mother, but we noticed things were completely different from the way we did things in Liberia. In Nigeria, the little ones would wait for the older ones to do things first. Take, for example, when it was time to use the washroom, the older ones would be first and the younger ones last, and the same when it came to eating and making decisions.

The first time we were given food to eat, they put ours all in a big bowl to eat together, and when we started to eat, Ukumaku—a girl who was around my age—told Chakakuka that he should eat first, and when he was done then I should eat, and when I was done Yahgahbo could eat, but we said to her that we don't do things like that in our country, we all eat together, younger ones and older ones.

She said that was total disrespect, and that even if she did allow her younger brother Junior to eat with her, he was not allowed to eat any meat unless she told him to. If at any time Junior disrespected her during the day when they were playing, when it was time for them to eat he was not going to be allowed to eat anything at all.

Ukumaku and I became very close friends and would talk about lots of things. Most times, we would go to visit her other friends and she would show me her neighbourhood and the different kinds of food they ate. One of my favourite foods was their beans-ikaria, which I loved to go and buy each time I got money. I was learning the different kinds of food they cooked and how to cook them by helping Ukumaku's older sisters in the kitchen.

Most mornings, they would make a certain food called cocoyam porridge or yam porridge. Sometimes they would cook the beans with palm oil with no meat in it with a stew on the side with boiled yam and fried plantain, and that would be breakfast. For dinner, we would eat pounded yam with peanut butter soup, or iba with egusee soup, or sometimes we would eat the iba with okra soup or with this special soup called abonnou.

Only occasionally would they ever cook rice to eat, because for them rice wasn't their country's staple food like ours, and we started to feel really homesick because we missed our traditional food, which is mostly rice cooked in lots of different ways. Because we felt sick and tired of the kind of food being given to us, we would eat some of it but take whatever was left and throw it on the rooftop of another house and pretend that we ate of it.

One day, Ukumaku took me to one of her friend's places. I can't remember her name, but her parents' house and yard were very big and had a swimming pool. I wished at that very moment my parents were the ones who owned it, and I just didn't want to leave, but the girl said to us that we could come by sometime and all swim together. Ukumaku said she would let me wear one of her swimsuits, and I was so looking forward to that day.

When I got home, I told my mother about how beautiful Ukumaku's friend's parents' house was, and she told me to be very careful where I go around Lagos as Nigerians were not to be trusted, but the next day, Chakakuka and Yahgahbo wanted to come along with Ukumaku and me. The next day we had so much fun; we forgot that it was getting late.

When we got home late, we all got a whipping and then we had to go and shower. We were still not sure how things were done in Nigeria, but we as little kids were asked to shower outside in the back of the yard with water in a bucket. Because we got home late and the outside lights in the backyard were turned off at a certain time of the night, we ended up taking a shower outside in the dark. We showered in pairs; all the girls showered together first then the boys showered after.

That night, we were not allowed to eat our evening meals because they said we all got home late. Well, thanks to Ukumaku's friend, we all had enough to eat before coming home. My mother noticed we didn't like the food and that we weren't eating very much, so most times she would take us out to a restaurant to buy food for us to eat, or sometimes she would bring us food and tell us to eat it in the room so that no one noticed.

One day, my mother took us out, and while in the taxi we saw Victoria Island. She said that when Michael Jackson came to Nigeria many years back, he visited there, and that one day she would have the chance to take us there to see what it looked like. From a distance, I could tell how beautiful it was and hoped that one day I would be given a chance to see what it looked like. My mother's love for Jehovah God was very great, but she was struggling with the battle of taking care of her kids.

So, whatever time she got to attend meetings at the Kingdom Hall of Jehovah's Witnesses, she took us along and always reminded us of how important it was that we get to know Jehovah God, because no matter where life took us he was always there for us, and always made a way for us to be taken care of. I remember my first time experiencing a bus ride there—I nearly fell off because it only slowed down for people to try to get on it, but it didn't come to a full stop, so when it was coming, my mother told us all to get ourselves ready to jump on the bus.

I was not sure how important it was to really be ready when the bus came and I almost fell out of the bus, and then I started screaming, saying, "Mama, I am falling out of the bus!" and my mother grabbed me and pulled me back into the moving bus. When I finally landed on my feet and was safe, I realized there was no place for me to sit, so my mother told Chakakuka to stand up and give me a seat. When my brother did, the entire bus got angry at him and told him that women are supposed to stand up for men and give them a place to sit.

In Nigeria, women are given no respect, because the nation is taught that it is because of a woman that sin entered into the world, so because of that, women are not to be respected. My mother was gone a lot; I'm not sure if she had any luck finding our stepfather, but sometimes when she came home we were all fast asleep. We also became friends with the property owner's kids, who used to love to come out and play with us.

Most times, we would wait until their mother had left the house, then we would go over to play because their mother didn't like other kids coming into her home to play, for fear that things would get destroyed when she was not around. That is why when we went over, we made sure not to destroy anything in the house.

Most times we would play Hide-and-Go-Seek, or sometimes we would play with their toys because they had so many, because their mother would travel and bring so many back. The boy's sister was a little bit selfish and didn't like to share her toys, so what we would usually do when she tried to be selfish was decide not to play with her, and then she would agree to share her toys.

As times went by and we kept going there to play, my friend Ukumaku told me that the boy had a crush on me and that he wanted me to be his girlfriend. For me it was fun to know that the property owner's son liked me, so that meant I was now allowed in their house whenever the mother was not around. The sister next to him did not like me very much, but she had no choice because her brother liked me, and that meant she could not stop me from coming over.

Then something happened: the sister started having a crush on Chakakuka, but my friend Ukumaku did not like that very much because Ukumaku had feelings for my brother, too, and when she learned the girl liked my brother Chakakuka, Ukumaku soon started to limit our friendship with the girl. Whenever we went over to play, Ukumaku would find a way to make problems with the girl, so her brother would punish her by sending her to the room for a nap and not allowing her to play with us; that way, Ukumaku got time to run around with Chakakuka.

Sometimes, Ukumaku would tell me to ask the boy for money so we could buy street food, and the boy would give me the money. Being the first child for his mother and the only boy, each time his mother left the house she would give him money just in case he needed to buy something. My friendship with the boy started to get really close, to the point where I would sneak out of the house and meet him upstairs in his mother's house when she was not around, or at the back of the yard.

Sometimes I would even ask my friend Ukumaku to watch out and let me know if someone was coming, and if there was, the boy would run upstairs to his house and Ukumaku and I would pretend to be playing. Just when we were starting to adjust, Ukumaku's father returned from his business trip and things changed quickly for us. Ukumaku's father was very upset with her mother for allowing us to stay in the house, and that confused his wife because she thought he would be happy that she helped his friend AmiShasi's woman and kids, but the guy wasn't pleased.

What we didn't know was that my mother and the guy were having an affair when the army sent him to keep peace in Liberia, so when my mother had brought us to his home to seek refuge, she had come up with the perfect plan by telling his wife that her husband and our stepfather were close friends.

Now that the guy was home, things weren't so well because the guy was uncomfortable in his own home, but we as kids didn't really know at the time what was really going on until the day my mother and the guy's older daughters got into a big fight, and the girl said to my mother that my mother lied to her family and came to ruin her parents' marriage. We were given a week to leave the house, but luckily for us my mother got in contact with a lady she knew and helped who was a sister at the Kingdom Hall of Jehovah's Witnesses, who once lived in Liberia but was now back in Nigeria with her kids.

The woman's name was Sepnah, and she had grown kids and some little ones. Her husband had died a while ago, making her a widow and a single mother. Because my mother helped this lady escape the war in Liberia, and also helped her many times to survive during the war, this lady agreed to help my mother by allowing us to move in with her and her kids until we could relocate to Ghana, where her brother was staying. Meanwhile, at Ukumaku's house, her family told the kids not to come near us or even talk or eat with us, and I must say that really did hurt a lot because Ukumaku and I were really close, and now we were not allowed to be friends any more.

It was not long until we moved out of Ukumaku's parents' house into my mother's friend Sepnah's house. When we arrived with all of our baggage, Sepnah invited us into her house and then called all her kids to come and greet us.

She had two girls around the same age as Yahgahbo and me, and two big boys. We were given one of the bedrooms in the house to share with my mother. I can remember that night: my mother and her friend talked for hours about when we all spent time together displaced at the Logan Town Kingdom Hall of Jehovah's Witnesses in Liberia, and also about how we all escaped and made it safe to Nigeria. We learned many things about the area from Sepnah's kids and what went on around there.

Once, they told us a story about an abandoned home opposite theirs. They told us that once there was a man who owned the place and he had lots of money, but one day armed robbers decided to pay him a visit after learning how much money he had. The armed robbers sent him a letter warning him that they were on their way to pay him a visit, and that he should get prepared to fight back. The man's wife warned him that they had to get out of there, but the man said he would not allow any local robbers to make him run from his own home, so the man decided to stay.

The day the armed robbers arrived, there were lots of gunshots exchanged, but in the end the armed robbers succeeded and got into the man's yard. After the armed robbers captured the man, they asked him why it was that he alone should have all that kind of money, and the man said, well, all fingers were not equal.

The armed robbers said to the man, "Well then, we are about to make them equal," and they took a knife, put the man's fingers on the table, and cut them equal. After, they said, "Now are they all equal?" However, the man was in so much pain he could not reply; the robbers took all his money and killed him and his family and with no one to claim the house it was left abandoned.

I remember the first time I had to follow Sepnah's daughter to buy some food to cook; I must say, it was an awesome experience for me. However, we did not get to go to the big market, but we managed to go to the nearby stores that sold foodstuffs. In Nigeria, everything is measured in kilograms, whereas in Liberia and other parts of the world things are measured in pounds. What I found amazing was that when you buy fish, which is measure in kilograms, they would clean the fish right in front of your face. The same goes for meat: when you buy it, they ask you what size you would like your meat cut into.

The same goes for onions and tomatoes: when you buy them, they get weighed in kilograms right in front of you and then they blend the onions and tomatoes for you. It was just so amazing and made it easy when you got home to cook, because all you had to do was wash what needed to be washed and then start cooking.

The lady who owned the store's son liked me, so whenever my mother would send us to buy foodstuffs and other things for the house, Sepnah's daughter and I would go over to the boy's mother's store to get the things we needed, and he would always give us extra stuff, but he would never really talk with me. The only thing I would find him doing was giving me a lot of smiles, but that would be it, until one day when he asked me for my name and I told him it's Arnelle, and he said his name was some very hard-to-pronounce Nigerian name.

After all these years I am still unable to pronounce or remember it, so he told me to call him Tim, as in short for Timothy. We became friends, but it would not be for long, because one day my mother came home and told us that she was working on getting us out of Nigeria so we could go to another West African country called Ghana. When my mother shared the news with her friend Sepnah, she wasn't too pleased that we would be leaving soon, because she thought my mother had a lot of money and didn't want to share it with her.

What she didn't know was that my mother met people who volunteered to help her get us out of Nigeria, and these friends of hers would buy stuff to keep that we would need on the road while travelling, including food. My mother's friend Sepnah decided she would no longer cook with us, and that her kids should not even come around for us to play with or to eat with anymore. Just before we could leave Nigeria, we were invited by some friends to a big party.

At first, my mother was afraid to let us go to the party alone without her supervision, but because it was not far from where we were staying, she agreed that we could go, but warned us not to follow strangers or allow anyone to give us something to drink. We agreed, and off to the party we went, but when we got to the place, it did not look much like a party from the outside. The house looked somehow unfinished because it was not painted.

When we entered the house it was a different story; the inside of the house was well furnished and beautiful, so we asked the woman of the house why the outside of the house was not fixed. She told us that they did that to avoid armed robbers, because once they see your house looking fancy on the outside, they think you have a lot of money and will come to steal from you. In the process, you could get hurt or killed.

I found that very smart and interesting, and though we came a bit too early, the lady gave us just a little bit of food to get us started, but we thought they didn't have even enough food to fill us. We wondered what kind of party this was without much to eat, and we decided to drink lots of water to make us feel full so that we didn't feel so bad for attending the party. To our surprise, as soon as we filled ourselves with water more food started to arrive at the party.

People were bringing food in barrels, and when we saw that we started to cry because there was no space left in our stomachs to put more food. We did not know that it was a non-stop seven-day party, meaning that you could go home, sleep a bit, come back, and the party was still going on. We were so mad, and we wished we had something to drink that could flush out our stomach so there could be space to eat more food.

We waited around so our food could digest. After a while, we were able to eat more food, but we could not be too long because my mother did not want us walking the streets late, because they were even worse at night. When it was time for us to leave, the woman told us we could take as much food home as we wanted, so we took enough food with us and some soft drinks and said thanks and left.

When we got home, we explained everything to my mother, telling her how greedy we were from the beginning and didn't know there was more food to come. She laughed at us and told us she should have warned us there was going to be lots of food at the party, because Nigerian parties are big. We talked all night, and finally my mother told us that she had something to tell us. She said it was good news.

She told us she had all of our papers ready for us to go to Ghana and that we would be leaving in two days, but that we should keep it a secret and not tell anyone until it was time. We did just as my mother instructed us, and the day before we could leave was when my mother told her friend Sepnah that we would be leaving early the next morning for Ghana. Sepnah started being nice and saying that she would miss us, and so would her kids, but we knew that was all a lie because she didn't act very nicely to us, and now that we were leaving she was going to miss us—yeah, right.

Nevertheless, we were very excited about leaving for Ghana, and when the evening came we could barely sleep. My mother told us to get some rest, that we would need it for the trip. My mother, as always, made sure she cooked some food that we could eat along the way, and made sure all our bags were packed and ready for our trip early the next morning. Off to bed we went, and before we knew it, it was time for us to wake up and get ourselves ready to go.

We were up by 4:00 a.m., because my mother said the bus for Ghana was leaving at 6:00 a.m. and her friend would be at the house at 5:00 to pick us up to give us a ride to the bus station. We were all dressed and ready to go, but then we noticed we were going to miss the friends we'd made, so we tried begging my mother to stay just one more day, but she insisted that she already made all arrangements for the day we going to leave and she didn't want to change them.

My mother's friend was over at 5:00 a.m. as promised; we all said our goodbyes to Sepnah and the kids, and off to the bus station we went. When we got to the bus stop, we were surprised to see that many people were also there awaiting their own time to travel.

Because we were up early and didn't have time to eat breakfast, my mother bought food from the ladies on the street so that we had something to eat before we left on the bus. She promised that once we were settled on the bus, she would give us some of the food she had prepared for the trip. It was time for us to get on the bus, so the bus driver called all the names of those who had already paid for their trip to Ghana.

My mother arranged the seating, making sure that we all sat very close to one another so that we felt safe and comfortable. After we were all seated and ready to leave, the bus driver turned off the lights and began to take off.

# CHAPTER 13

# OUR TRIP TO GHANA: THE LAND THAT BECAME OUR HOME

Just as the bus was about to take off, my mother held our hands and began to say a prayer to Jehovah God, asking him to please guide us and protect us from any trouble that may come our way, and to please lead us to safety. On the trip to Ghana, we saw many places and we experienced the ways other people lived.

Most of the trip we slept in the bus, because it would just go. The driver was trying to cross the major immigration checkpoints, but when it came time to stop so everyone could get down to use the washroom, my mother would wake us up. When we were done, she would buy us some of the food the ladies were selling on the streets and we would also eat some of the food she made.

Then we'd be up and surprised to see the different places, and we would point them out to my mother and she would explain to us what some of those places represented and why some of them were isolated. The trip was a bit long, but we finally made it to Ghana, and though the place looked different, I was willing to learn about my new environment. The bus reached its final stop: a marketplace called Kaneshi in Accra, Ghana.

We all got off the bus and my mother made sure that none of us was missing. She warned us to all stay together so that we did not get lost, because it was a place she herself was unfamiliar with. She looked for the bus we would take to the Liberian refugee camp, a place where she learned her brother Sokoka stayed, but she wasn't a hundred percent sure.

I was dying to use the washroom. I asked my mother where I could urinate and she told me to ask around, but when I asked and someone showed me where the washroom was, the line was too long and I didn't know what else to do. I went back to my mother, confused, and did not know what to do, and told her the line was too long and I would not be able to wait. My mother told me to go find somewhere to urinate, but everywhere I went was someone's business area and they would chase me away. I got frustrated and just stood up and urinated on myself, and what made it worse was that I was wearing a very light blue jean, so everyone around noticed what happened to me. They came around to ask my mother if I was OK and whether I had bladder problems. My mother explained to them that I didn't have a bladder problem, it was just that I had kept my urine for a long time during the trip and that I couldn't hold it anymore.

Even with so many people around, my mother took my clothes off, left me only in my panties, went into the luggage and brought out a clean set of clothes for me. I was feeling all nice and dry afterwards, but I was ashamed that I had to change my clothes in front of the entire world. The bus that was to take us to the Liberian refugee camp finally arrived, and at that time it was getting a bit late but we managed to get on the bus, along with all of our luggage.

The bus was very overcrowded, and the ride took two to three hours with all the traffic on the road from Kaneshi to Buduburam Liberian refugee camp. We finally arrived and it looked like a place I didn't wish to be at, but who was I to say anything? I went along wherever my mother took me, and I just wanted to be somewhere safe, and wherever that was is where I was happy to be.

My mother went around the Liberian refugee camp asking where she could find her brother Sokoka, and someone who knew where he lived told my mother that he stayed at the Buduburam village not far from the Liberian refugee camp. The person told my mother it would take a few minutes to walk there. We were so tired we could barely walk, but we had to manage.

We had our luggage carried in a wheelbarrow to the village. When we finally made it to where the person claimed my Uncle Sokoka lived, it was a very small hut with a room as big as a kitchen, and I said to myself, *How were we all going to fit in here?* When my Uncle Sokoka heard the sound of his sister's voice, it became the happiest night of his life, because he had not seen her in years. When we met my Uncle Sokoka, he and his girlfriend Almona had just had a bouncing baby boy, and they had Almona's sister Prikar staying there, too, but not in the same room.

She had a room she rented from a Ghanaian in the village, so my Uncle Sokoka and his girlfriend Almona decided that my mother would share the room with Prikar. That night, none of us wanted to fall asleep; we sat up talking for hours, but when it was finally time for us to sleep, my mother put some blankets on the floor, because Prikar's bed was not big enough for all of us to sleep on.

The next morning, we woke up to sounds of sweeping outside; we didn't know that in Ghana it is traditional for them to sweep their home and outside yard very early in the morning, and they have a certain way of sweeping that makes a design when they are done. I remember that early morning; when we woke, my mother was already up and having a chat with her brother Sokoka about the rest of the family and about the war and about friends and family that died during it.

We asked my mother where we could brush our teeth and take a shower; my mother told us to take cups of water, put some toothpaste on our toothbrushes, and brush our teeth behind the house. It was strange brushing behind the house with people walking by watching us.

We asked my mother where we could take a shower. She said there was a little place behind the house with rocks on the floor and curtains for a door. She told us to go into the room, put on our towels, and meet her behind the house, where she would meet us with a hot bucket of water. She also told us to make sure to bring the African Net Scrubber and the soap dish along with us. My mother would stand and wait for us to wash our skin, but Prikar told her that the place was safe and that it was OK to leave us alone to scrub ourselves.

My mother told us that it was OK to scream for her if we felt unsafe, and the room was just a minute's walk from the place we took our bath. After washing our skin, we went into the room, put lotion on our skin, and put on clothes. When we came out of the room, we realized that the Ghanaian women in the village put baby powder around their necks and other places as their way of smelling good. We only put baby powder on at night so that we smelled fresh, but not during the day.

That morning, Almona fried eggs with bread and made Ovaltine. After I helped her give the baby his bottle and change his diapers, Almona got ready for us to go to the market. The road to the market seemed confusing, but I was willing to learn how to get there. When we got to the marketplace, there were some market ladies who knew Almona and asked her who the new girl was, and she responded by saying I am her boyfriend's niece who just came from Nigeria along with her mother, brother, and sister.

Some of the women greeted me, and some were too busy trying to sell their foodstuffs. Almona showed me the prices of everything, how to bargain with the women at the market, and how to make sure that I was being given the right change.

She also showed me where I could go to buy big chicken feet, because she said that my Uncle Sokoka loves them very much and that he would not eat the food unless there was chicken feet in it. I'm not sure what she cooked that day, but I am sure we all enjoyed it to the fullest.

Almona and my Uncle Sokoka had a Liberian neighbour, and although I forgot their names, I still remember the name of the kid's mother: Korpo. They would cook Torburgee every day.

Every soup these people cooked would be Torburgee. I have never seen people eat as much baking soda as this family. They cooked Torburgee so much that their tongues were cooked from the baking soda, making their English more difficult to pronounce and harder to understand. Sometimes when they talked, we would laugh because their English sounded so funny, but in no time we became fast friends.

When Korpo sent one of her daughters to the market, they would come and ask me if I was ready to go with them, and then I would ask my mother or Almona or Prikar, depending on who was cooking that day, if they were ready for me to go to the market. My mother taught Almona how to cook for more than just a day, but Almona claimed that Uncle Sokoka doesn't like leftovers and that is why she cooked a new meal each day.

If you ask me, I love the idea very much because I like to eat new food, and if she's willing to cook every day I am in, plus I don't mind going to the market, which is at the Liberian refugee camp; it allowed me to learn my way around the camp better. Each time Korpo sent one of her daughters to the market, they would come over to ask me if I was ready to go, then either my mother or Almona or Prikar would give me money and a list of things they wanted me to buy.

Each time we would cook, there would always be chicken feet in the food because Uncle Sokoka liked them. Once the food started to cook, Uncle Sokoka would put music on for us all to dance to, and when he danced it was like he was jogging, so we would tease him by calling him chicken feet because he loved them so much. Almona started trusting me to take care of her baby Alex. My duties where to change the baby's diapers, feed him, and put him to bed. And when I say feed him, that means I was in charge of the food and the feeding.

Almona always bought this expensive milk for her son called Nido milk, so when I was given the job of being the baby's caregiver, I didn't complain because I knew that me and baby Alex would be sharing that milk equally. Every time Chakakuka and Yahgahbo wanted to help care for the baby, I would refuse and say Almona asked only me alone to do the work, until one day I was caught by Chakakuka eating the baby food. He threatened to report me, so I promised him that we would share the food together.

We would make the baby food and give it to him, then we would make our own in two separate cups. Almona noticed her baby food was starting to finish faster than the expected date. When she asked us why the baby food seemed to finish faster than expected, we would tell her that her baby ate a lot. That went on for a while, until one day Prikar came into the room to get something.

Apparently, Prikar had been calling us to get her cooking spoon from the room and we did not hear her, so she came to get it herself and that is when she caught us helping ourselves to the baby Alex's food. She said, "I knew it, I knew you guys have been up to something because of the way you guys argue and fight over who is going to feed the baby."

She said to us, "Come outside so I can let your mother Deborah and Almona know what you guys have been up to." When Prikar told Almona and my mother what we had been doing, Almona said, "I see why my son's food been finishing faster than normal, and from now on you guys are not allowed to feed my son together, only one person will be allowed to do that and that person will be Arnelle, and I am going to make sure I measure my son's milk and food before giving it to her."

I was very mad at Chakakuka, and I told him, "You see, if you had been watching we wouldn't have been caught." From then on, Almona started measuring her son's food to make sure we weren't eating any of it. The old woman who Prikar rented from became fond of me and started teaching me how to cook their traditional Ghanaian food called Banku and Kanky. She usually made it for the market days at Kasioa, Tuesday and Friday.

We started to wrap the Banku and Kanky on early Monday mornings, and we would get done very late Monday night for Tuesday's market day, and then on Wednesday she would take the fermented corn to the corn mill and have it ground. Once she got home, she would put water on it to let it ferment a bit more before wrapping it on Thursday for market day on Friday. Each time the old lady would make her traditional Ghanaian food, she would give me some to eat, and because my mother liked Banku and Kanky, she didn't mind me helping the old lady out.

My mother would sometimes buy some from the old lady, but most times she would just wait until I got mine then she would make pepper sauce for it, sometimes with sardines or fried fish, and then she would give us some and keep the rest for herself, Almona, and Prikar. Sometimes my Uncle Sokoka would eat some, too, because he liked the way my mother made it for them. When it was time for my mother to cook, she would put so much meat in the food, and this would make Uncle Sokoka very happy because his sister liked to cook lots of food.

One day my mother decided to cook our traditional Liberian food called cassava gravy.

At the time I didn't know that I had an allergy to cassava, so after my mother was done the cooking, I took my share of the food and started to eat. As I ate, I started to have trouble breathing.

My mother thought at first that someone in the village had bewitched me, but Uncle Sokoka, who was there at the time of the asthma attack, told my mother what it was, and he told her what kind of medicine I would need. She found it hard to believe that her daughter was actually asthmatic, so she took me to the clinic on the Buduburam Liberian refugee camp and it was confirmed that it was indeed an asthma attack.

So, my mother bought Ventolin tablets, because the Ventolin inhaler was too expensive. The tablets work the same but they take longer to start working, whereas a puffer starts to work immediately. My mother was still confused, and told me that from then on I should make sure to keep myself warm, not to play in the dust too much, and that I was no longer allowed to eat cassava, because she didn't want me having another attack.

As we started to adjust to the refugee life and make new friends, it was time for school. My mother registered us at the Buduburam Liberian refugee school. She registered Chakakuka and me in Grade Six, but I can't remember what grade Yahgahbo was in. My mother got all of our school supplies, including uniforms, and within a week we started school.

I was excited and scared, because what if the kids at school were not nice to me? What if they laughed at me? But most of all I was just excited to be starting school. Before we started, I had to get my hair done in a way that would show me off as the new hot girl in school. I had my hair braided in a way that would make it shake when I ran and when I walked. My hair was natural and long, and I used to spend a lot of time taking care of it.

The day came and we started school. I remember that my mother made sure that we showered the night before, so that we did not delay getting ready for school in the morning. All we had to do was brush our teeth and put on our uniforms. In our backpack, there was lunch already made for us but still my mother gave us spending money just in case we needed to buy extra stuff.

At school, we had to stand on what was called the division line, which was a line that each class would form in the morning to say prayers, sing the school oath, salute the flag, and hear school announcements. While on the line, I made some new friends who promised to show me around, but I cannot remember their names. Even though there were two Grade Six classes, Chakakuka and I ended up sitting in the same class.

I was seated with my new friends at the back of the class, which is normally where most of the disrespectful students sat. Chakakuka started to make new friends, too, and we began to adjust. The teacher came into the class and asked each person to introduce themselves with their names and where they were from.

When it was my turn, I said my name was Arnelle, and I told the class that we had recently come from Nigeria to live with our uncle and his family on the refugee camp, and the entire class became interested and wanted to know more, but there wasn't enough time for all of that. Chakakuka introduced himself as well, and told them a little bit about our travel to Ghana. Soon we had many friends at lunchtime who were interested in getting to know more about our trip.

During the lunch hour, I went with my friends to meet with Yahgahbo, who told me about her morning and how she made new friends. I told her to meet us at our class after school so we could all walk home together, and off with my friends I went. They took me for a walk into parts of the refugee camp, and before we knew it, it was time for us to return to school because our lunch break was almost over. We hurried back as fast as we could, but we were still late entering the class.

I can't remember the name of the teacher we met in class that day, but as soon as we walked in, he called the class's attention to us and said, "Today is the first day of school and we are all getting to know one another, so I am not going to punish you guys right away, but if this behaviour gets repeated, there will be punishment awaiting you all." We took our seats, and for the rest of the day we all introduced ourselves to the teachers and the teachers did the same and told us what subject they would be teaching.

Each teacher that came to class gave us the subject books we would need to study. We were to take them home and bring the book of whatever subject would be taught that day, so by the time the day was over we had a lot of books to take home, along with the books we would be using to write in. The school day ended, and it was time for us all to go home and prepare for school the next day.

By then, we were familiar with most of our classmates' names. Yahgahbo met us at our class door and we all walked home together. On our way, we talked about our day and the friends we made.

# CHAPTER 14

# A NEW BOY AT SCHOOL

After a few months of school at the Liberian Buduburam refugee camp, we got an announcement that a new boy would be joining our Grade Six class, and that he was from the United States of America. Wow, I get to have a boy from the United States of America as a classmate? I just could not wait to see what he looked like. The next day was his first day of school, and when he was brought to our class, the teacher seated him next to me; it was as if the teacher could read my mind.

Damn, the boy was cute, and he had a beautiful chocolate complexion. It was because he once lived in very good weather conditions; it had given him a very good skin tone. The teacher asked him to stand and introduce himself, and when he stood up, all my attention was on him. I watched the way he talked and how good his English was—more American English, though. His lips were pink, he had a purple backpack, and he brought his video games with him. I believe it was Nintendo, but the teacher told him that in African schools we do not allow them in the classroom.

He introduced himself as Vicker and told the class that he wouldn't be in Africa much longer, that his mom sent him for vacation and that he would return in six months to America. But we all knew that when a parent sends their kid to Africa, it's because that kid had been behaving rudely and they were sent back to experience the African life and get African discipline, so we all knew he wasn't going back anytime soon.

When asked what subjects he was good at, he said math and English, and the class laughed because we studied thirteen subjects and one had to be good at all of them if they wanted to pass into the next class. He said in America you only had to study the subjects you were good at. Every girl in the class had a crush on Vicker, and all the boys wanted to be friends with him, but he befriended Chakakuka because he was mixed Lebanese and Liberian and that made Vicker comfortable, because Chakakuka reminded him of the friends he once had in America.

Chakakuka, on the other hand, found the perfect opportunity to play Vicker's video games. My brother did not want Vicker to be friends with anyone at the school; he just wanted to be Vicker's only friend so he would have the opportunity to share whatever Vicker had brought from America. Chakakuka was not so good at math and English and he needed Vicker to help him; Vicker, on the other hand, was not good with science and other subjects, and he needed Chakakuka for that.

They planned to be study friends, and when I asked to join, Chakakuka refused, not wanting me to be a part of their study plan, so I studied by myself. Chakakuka knew I had a crush on Vicker, but he didn't like his friends coming around Yahgahbo and me.

Each time I would try to visit them during lunchtime, he would tell Vicker that they were going to sit or play somewhere else. It hurt me a little, but I had my own friends so I let Chakakuka be while I hung out with them.

At school, there was a talent search to join drama, music, dance, and other programs, so I joined the drama, music, and dance classes.

It pleased me to learn that Vicker joined the dance and music classes as well; it was the perfect opportunity to show him I had talent and that I could dance and sing. Later, I learned that my mother was good friends with Vicker's family and sometimes she would send me over to deliver stuff. When I got there, I would ask for Vicker and I remember one of his aunties asking him if I was his new girl, but he didn't say anything, he only smiled, and that kind of excited me.

Now that I knew where Vicker's family was staying in the refugee camp, I would visit and help every other day. Even when my mother sent me to the market, I would get Vicker so we could walk to the market together. Chakakuka started spending less time with Vicker; he was getting concerned but did not yet know that Vicker and I were hanging out. Vicker's mother called from the United States and gave her family a strong warning concerning Vicker, that they were not allowed to spoil him and that her reason for sending him there was for him to get serious discipline.

Vicker's relatives started making him go to the market to buy household food and make sure there was enough water in the house for cooking and showering. Vicker would use a five-gallon wheelbarrow to fetch water for his household, but even with that, it was a huge struggle for him because he was not used to that kind of life.

People in the Liberian refugee camp who knew that Vicker was from the United States would laugh very hard when they saw Vicker struggling with the water in the wheelbarrow. They would say aloud, "Isn't this the American boy pushing the wheelbarrow? He is now becoming African." Vicker would get very mad, but there was not much he could do. Each time his mother phoned, Vicker would tell her that he didn't like the life in the Liberian refugee camp and that he would like to come back home to the United States, and his mother would lie to him saying she was coming to get him soon.

Chakakuka still hung out with Vicker, but not as much because he had made other new friends and was finding Vicker a bit boring once he learned that all the things he brought with him from the United States were stolen. Vicker's mother was not coming to get him anytime soon, and he started to feel that the less time he spent with Vicker was the more time I would. We would go almost everywhere together, and I helped show him around the refugee camp.

I was not spending much time studying and would sometimes forget that I had schoolwork to complete. Vicker's family attended the Kingdom Hall of Jehovah's Witnesses, same as us, and that led to more distraction for me because I was always wanting to get my hair done to make sure it looked nice. My mother didn't say much about it all, she was waiting for our school progress reports to come then she would make her decision.

The time came and the school reports were in, and we had to take them home ourselves and hand them over to our parents. When I saw my report card, I was so worried that I did not even want to go home, because I know my mother would be truly disappointed.

Chakakuka's report card wasn't all that bad, and neither was Yahgahbo's, but mine was the worst. Before I could get home to show it to my mother, Chakakuka and Yahgahbo had already given her the news, so my mother was just waiting for me to come home. When I got home, my mother Deborah was so mad at me I could see it in her eyes. She said to me, "I won't beat you as you are expecting me to, I am going to send you to the barber shop and have all your hair shaved off, then next time you will be serious about your schoolwork and will stay focused in school."

My heart broke when my mother said that as I'd never had my hair cut or shaved before, so all I wanted to do was run away, but where would I run to? My mother told me to put my backpack down, and she gave Chakakuka money so that the barber could shave my hair off, and it all seemed too much fun for Chakakuka and he couldn't wait for my head to be shaved.

From the time I left the house until the time we arrived at the barbershop, I was crying and begging Chakakuka to beg our mother for me, but he was too excited to see my hair shaved off. We finally arrived at the barbershop, and the barber could see me crying bitterly and asked why I was crying. I told him it was because I didn't want to get my hair cut or shaved, and the barber said to me that my hair was too long, and it made him afraid to put scissors in it.

He told Chakakuka to take me back home and tell my mother that there were other punishments she could give me for not making good grades, but he was not comfortable cutting my hair, especially hair this long. Before I knew it, my brother had taken the scissors to the front of my head at the very roots of my hair and put the scissors right through it.

My heart broke into a million pieces to see Chakakuka do that to me instead of protecting and defending me. I got very mad, and then the barber said to me, "Well, there is nothing I can do now. From the way your brother cut your hair, I would have to shave your hair low to make it even." So, the barber went on to cut my hair, and as he did it I cried hard and hated Chakakuka and my mother for humiliating me.

As I walked out of the barber shop, everyone started to laugh at me and I ran all the way home crying, and when I got home, my mother said, "This is what you get for not paying attention in class, and the next time you fail, your punishment will be worse than this. I could not believe my mother made me look like a boy, and Chakakuka and Yahgahbo could not stop laughing at me.

Sometimes Chakakuka would even knock my head, and when I cried about it to my mother she would pretend to be advising Chakakuka not to do it again, but then she, too, would laugh about it and I would just go into the room and cry all by myself, and sometimes even refuse to eat anything. The day came and it was time to return to school, and Chakakuka found so much joy in knowing that I was going to be laughed at and he could not wait to see what the class was going to say.

I got to school very late and it was hard for me to go to class; fear took hold of me and I did not know what to expect, especially with Vicker being in the same class. When I finally arrived in class, my lateness brought more attention to me and the entire class got a really good laugh. They all knew I had a crush on Vicker, and said to him, "Look, your girl is now a boy!" Vicker laughed at me, too, and he started to avoid me and became friends with some other girl. I can't remember what her name was, but I didn't get his attention anymore.

The hurt and pain I felt from losing my hair and the humiliation at school got me to join a study class after school and put in more time on my homework. My grades became better than my brother's and sister's, so my mother asked them why their grades weren't as good as mine.

Though we were busy in school, we still took time after school before studying to look after Uncle Sokoka's baby Alex. Alex was growing very fast and getting big; everyone in the Buduburam village knew Alex and was in love with him. All he could do was stand at that time; he was not walking yet, but one weekend when I was taking care of him something happened. Alex realized for the first time that he had a shadow and he was amazed that his shadow was doing whatever he was.

When Alex moved his leg, his shadow would move its leg, too, so Alex decided to follow his shadow. Alex did not realize that he had started walking; he chased his shadow across the street to the neighbour's house and then back home. Everyone was happy that night, knowing that Alex could walk now, but this also meant extra work, because now it was unsafe to let him wander around. Walking kids might look slow, like they can't go far, but they can go far very quickly.

The next thing we knew, Alex was in every neighbour's house, and sometimes it would take us thirty minutes to find him because we would go from house to house asking for him. But the good thing was that everyone in the village knew him, and sometimes one of the villagers would find him at their house and they would feed him and bring him home. Alex became fond of a lady in the village named Mimi, and he would go over to her place all the time for a visit, so whenever we looked for Alex, we would go over to Mimi's place first.

Mimi had her boyfriend, or, let me say, lover, and as little Alex was only a year old, he would get mad and jealous when Mimi's man would come over for visit, and he would refuse to let us bring him home. Mimi would tell us to leave him there and that she would bring him later. She would sometimes joke that Alex was her little husband, and when Alex finished his feeding and shower he would go right over to Mimi's house. Sometimes Almona would give Mimi extra diapers and clothes for him to get changed into in case he needed it. Sometimes Alex would not know that Mimi was not home, and he would go over to find the door closed, and knock.

My Uncle Sokoka was attending school at the university in Ghana, and they had a contest where the person who wrote the best English essay got sent to Canada for schooling. Therefore, he came home and told Almona, my mother Deborah, and Prikar about it and said he was going to try.

My Uncle Sokoka would study for hours by candlelight, just so he could win the contest so his family could get a better life away from the refugee camp and away from the war in Liberia. Meanwhile, my mother would warn us not to make noise, because Uncle Sokoka needed to concentrate. Uncle Sokoka submitted his English essay for the contest, and they had to wait a month or two to get the results in.

We were all praying that it was possible for Uncle Sokoka to win the English essay contest, but while waiting we still went on with our day-to-day activities. The day came and the results were in, and luckily for us, Uncle Sokoka came first place. We were all happy, because we knew soon Uncle Sokoka would be going to Canada and life would be a bit easier for us now.

A few months later, Uncle Sokoka was set to go to Canada to study, and it was sad watching him go but we all knew it was for the better. It was very early in the morning when Uncle Sokoka had to leave, but my mother still managed to wake us all up so we could say goodbye and wish him a safe trip.

We were unable to go, but my mother, Almona, and Prikar took him to the airport. When they returned to the refugee camp, I knew for sure that my Uncle Sokoka had left for Canada. My mother was feeling a bit sad, but Almona was crying because she'd spent so much time with him and wasn't used to being apart.

Prikar comforted her, saying that everything was going to be OK; now that Uncle Sokoka was staying in Canada, Almona wouldn't have anything to worry about. A week after Uncle Sokoka arrived, he phoned letting us know that he had arrived and that everything was OK. He also mentioned that the place was very cold, and told us of his first time experiencing snow, and what the country looked like.

Uncle Sokoka promised to send us some money to take care of our well-being until he could manage to send for all of us. As months went by, things were OK with my Uncle Sokoka gone and able to send some money for the family, but things didn't stay that way for too long. I'm not sure what happened, but things started to get bad between my mother and Almona. They were not as close as they were when my Uncle Sokoka was with us.

Uncle Sokoka would call and try to settle things between my mother and Almona, but things still weren't working as they should. Almona wanted her freedom and my mother thought it was her duty to make sure she kept an eye on Almona for her brother. Things in the Liberian refugee camp started to get bad. Ghana started to suffer from drought, and water everywhere started to get very expensive. It got to the point where we had to go to another village just to get water for washing clothes and cooking.

All of us had to wake up as early as 5:00 to go to a village called Sayanbreku, which was well known for its voodoo and witchcraft. I'm not sure how many hours' walk it was from the Buduburam village to the Sayanbreku village, but it took forever to get there. Even though the walk required a lot of endurance, it seemed fun because many people from the Buduburam Liberian refugee camp and from the Buduburam village were also on their way to the same village.

We needed to learn the rules of the Sayanbreku village, so while we were on our way, we began to ask people what their rules were and what to expect when we got there. Those that had been there before told us to be very careful and to show everyone respect, because we did not know who was who and who had power to do us harm. They also explained to us about the rules of the place we were all going to get water from.

They told us that we would have to leave our footwear a few blocks away before getting to the creek to get water, because the villagers believe that the ground around the creek is holy and one must not take their footwear there. There would be punishment for anyone who disobeyed the rules.

Some of the punishment might be that the person would disappear once entering the water with their footwear and never get to see their family ever again, so my mother warned us strongly not to forget it once we were there. The distance was far and looked a bit scary as we walked along the road. The people we met along the way to the Sayanbreku gave us information we would need as to how to get to the village since we had never been there before.

As we walked, we took breaks to rest for a bit and then we would continue. We finally got to the Sayanbreku village. When we got there, we still had to ask people where the creek was; some didn't understand English, but the ones who did directed us to the creek. We followed all the rules about getting to the creek, and when we got there the water was all muddy and dirty, but my mother insisted we still collect it. When we got to the Buduburam village, she would put chlorine in it to make it safe. I looked at the water and said to myself, *How the hell is the water going to get clean after being so dirty?*

I was only asking myself this because I had never seen how chlorine works before. We got the water we needed and started to head back to the Buduburam village, but it seemed like it took longer to get back than it did to get there.

When we returned to the village, my mother put chlorine into the water and spun it. As the water spun, it started to get clear and clean and all the dirt and mud started to settle to the bottom of the bucket.

My mother took another bucket and a clean white cloth and laid the cloth over the bucket. She instructed us to pour the water into the bucket through the white cloth, and as we poured the water into the bucket everything that we couldn't see in the water settled on the white cloth.

After straining the water, my mother took the water and boiled it so that it was safe to cook with and easier to wash with. We had to manage the water carefully because it was difficult to get, and we were not planning to go back to the Sayanbreku village to get water. We managed for a few days, and then things started to get back to normal with our water situation because it started to rain, so we put tubs, buckets, and barrels under the roof so that we could collect the water from the raindrops.

We collected enough water to last us for a week or two, depending on how we intended to use it. The government of Ghana also started to send water to the camp and the village, so water was not so expensive anymore. In addition, because there was no direct running water through taps, most people had a water reservoir, which can be built in many different ways. For example, in the Buduburam Liberian refugee camp, they used rubber water tanks as their water reservoir, and in the Buduburam village they used both rubber water tanks and a water reservoir built into the ground with cement.

They charged per bucket for water both in the camp and in the village, and the more water you needed the more it was going to cost you, but we were doing well for water, because whenever it rained we used up what we needed and then saved the rest of the water. Being friends with Korpo's kids, we learned about other things that people could eat, such as a Liberian bug called bug-a-bug, and I also learned that Korpo and her family ate grasshoppers. I remember the very first time I ate a bug-a-bug; it was one night while it was raining and there were lots of bugs under the light. When I tried to get rid of them, Korpo's kids said no, the bugs were good for eating and that they in fact taste like peanuts, so I wanted to learn how to catch them and how to cook them so that they are safe to eat.

Korpo's kids told me to put some water in the tub and then wet my hands, and then with a wet hand go under the light and try to catch the bugs. The purpose of wetting your hand is so that when it touches the bugs, the wetness of your hand would wet their wings making them unable to fly, and then you put the bugs in the tub of water after catching them so that they do not fly off. Once you have enough bugs, you can then drain out the water and put the bugs into a cooking pot and begin cooking them. While they are cooking you can add salt to give them their natural flavour.

Because the bugs have their own natural oil, all you need to do is put them in a pot with some heat and you are good to go, and as the bugs begin to cook their wings fall off. Chakakuka and Yahgahbo were also in on it, and when the bugs were well cooked, which we made sure they were, we tried them and they tasted very good. We wanted more but we hadn't caught enough to last, so Korpo's kids gave us some of theirs, and by the next day we couldn't wait for it to rain so we could collect more bugs.

The next thing Korpo's kids taught me was how to catch grasshoppers, but I was not interested in eating them, I only wanted to help and learn. The grasshoppers are very smart creatures, and to catch them one has to be very quiet, calculate well, and be fast as well. The poop from the grasshopper smells very bad, and if you were in a rush to catch it you could end up crushing it hard enough to get its poop all over your hands.

I learned how to catch them, and when we did, we took off their wings so that they would not fly off. We would go in the morning and sometimes return in the late afternoon. I made sure not to share food with them on the days I knew their mother Korpo was cooking the grasshoppers. What Korpo did was clean them nicely and put the clean dead grasshoppers up on the roof of their house to dry, and then cooked them.

I do not know what they found tasty about grasshoppers, but I never did try and still have not, and I am still not interested in them. We had a half-Ghanaian, half-Liberian neighbour staying in the village next to us whose name was Fanta. Fanta had a little boy name Freddy. Fanta was a very busy single mother who loved her son very much; I cannot remember how old Freddy was, but he was learning how to talk so probably around two to three years of age.

Freddy really liked Chakakuka; his mother made Chakakuka Freddy's personal care person when she went to work, and my brother loved that because Freddy's mother would always cook and leave delicious meals for him to feed Freddy with, but Chakakuka and Freddy would end up eating his food fifty-fifty. Chakakuka liked the idea of being Freddy's personal care person very much. Fanta was a very busy woman who would go to the market very early in the morning to braid women's hair for money, and Freddy was her only child.

Fanta was very close to us, and sometimes Freddy would sleep over and his mom knew where he was, but one day while Fanta was at work, Freddy went missing. We searched all over the village for Freddy and couldn't find him; oh, how worried Chakakuka was until one of the villagers found

Freddy and asked him where he was from. Being so young, Freddy couldn't talk very well but he pointed, and the villager brought him home.

Since that day, Chakakuka made sure Freddy was always by his side, and if Freddy was playing he would make sure he watched his every move. If he had to go somewhere, he would beg me to please watch Freddy for him. As months went by, my mother and Almona weren't getting along much, so Almona told my Uncle Sokoka that she would be moving to her godmother's place somewhere in town with the baby. When that happened, I missed them both very much.

I was too young to get myself involved in big people's business. Prikar and my mother continued to live together in the village. We moved into the hut, and my mother and Prikar shared their original room. They got along pretty well and would always go out either in the camp or in the city, Accra; when they returned, they would be up until morning talking about their night.

We moved into the hut, but when my mother and Prikar went out they asked us to sleep in their room, because apparently the Ghanaian villager they were renting the room from had a spare key to their room, and when no one was paying attention, the lady who my mother and Prikar rented from would go into their room and steal stuff, including cream and perfume. But one day she was caught by my mother, and they really got into it and it resulted in a fight. After that day, my mother and Prikar changed the lock but they still weren't sure if they could trust her.

Apparently, one night while my mother and Prikar were out, my mother met a man called Mr. Nana who we would later find more details about. We did not get to meet him just yet, but we would hear our mother and Prikar talk about him at night when they returned. One night, my mother went out and did not come home, and in the morning when we woke, we asked Prikar why our mother was not home, and Prikar replied that she had slept over at her friend's place.

Later on that day, my mother returned home but it was with a male friend driving an expensive car. This turned out to be Mr. Nana. They brought many foodstuffs with them for the house. Mr. Nana was a very good-looking man and I could see why my mother was very much in love with him, but there was a problem.

He was married, but he was very kind to us. I'm not sure if it was because he was crazy about my mother, but that day he gave us money and told us to get ourselves whatever we wanted. My mother wouldn't say a word about him giving us money until he left, then she called us and told us to give the money to her. I willingly gave my money to my mother, but Chakakuka and Yahgahbo frowned and said they wanted to keep theirs.

My mother soon made a new friend called Gegek, and they became fast friends in no time; Prikar did not like that very much, but still the three of them started to hang out. Now everything was about Mr. Nana, and we learned that he had kids, too, and soon my mother started to bring Mr. Nana's kids over for visits. Because we lived in the village and they lived in the city and attended international school, they carried themselves with a lot of attitude.

My mother would take Mr. Nana's daughters to the salon to get their hair and nails done and would leave us out. Prikar started hanging out with some of her friends from the Liberian refugee camp and was spending less time in the village. My mother started having so much fun that she was not around very much; we were left with Prikar to take care of us. Prikar was the one making sure we ate and showered and that everything was OK with us.

Later, my mother learned that Almona was cheating with one of her godmother's family members, and when my mother confronted her, they got into it and things did not end up well. Apparently, Almona was aware that my mother was dating Mr. Nana and learned that he was married, so Almona told my mother that she would go and let Mr. Nana's wife know what was happening.

Almona said she would tell Mr. Nana's wife that my mother was having a relationship with her husband. My mother didn't realize that Almona told Mr. Nana's wife about her relationship with him, but one day while my mother and Mr. Nana were hanging out at the camp, Mr. Nana's wife came and jumped my mother for a fight, but my mother managed to get out of there and come home.

We were unaware of all of this until the next morning, but that evening when my mother was home Mr. Nana came to visit her and ended up sleeping over and didn't return home. The next morning, his wife came to the camp to ask where my mother lived, and somebody directed her to the village. When she came to ask about my mother, we told her she wasn't home.

The lady saw her husband's car parked outside, so she knew my mother was home and that her husband was there, so she got very loud and started cursing, saying that she was not going anywhere and that she would wait until her husband came out. Mr. Nana's wife waited for a while, and when she got tired of waiting, she said to tell Mr. Nana that she would meet him at home, and to tell my mother that it was not over yet between them.

After she left, it took a while before Mr. Nana came out of the room because he was not sure if his wife had truly left. When Prikar came home, my mother explained what had happened, how all the villagers were paying attention and talking about her and how she didn't care, and if Mr. Nana's wife had taken better care of her husband, he wouldn't have left his mansion to come visit her in the village. However, the problem with married men who cheat is that they were born to be unfaithful, so just him cheating with another woman did not mean his wife had a problem.

If she did, he would not have married her and made her his wife. After that day, Mr. Nana no longer parked his car near our house, he drove somewhere in the village and parked then walked to our house to see my mother. My mother was taking a trip—to where I did not know at the time—and she asked Prikar to please watch over us and make sure we were OK, gave her some money to take care of us, and then she left for her trip.

Apparently, my mother went on a month-long trip with Mr. Nana, and we were left with a lot of food. The food started to run out, and Prikar started using the money her mother would send her from America to help take care of us. My mother came back with many stories about her trip and how much fun it was. She brought back things for Prikar, and for us as well. Mr. Nana's mother came to Ghana to visit from Liberia to help with Mr. Nana's kids and spend time with her son.

I'm not sure if the family did not like Mr. Nana's wife, but it was strange when I saw that Mr. Nana's mother liked my mother. I was very surprised. We had not known her for long, but there was a plan we did not know about. My mother had planned that when Mr. Nana's mother returned to Liberia, she would take us along and we would stay at her house until she returned to Liberia to get us.

Our transportation was arranged and paid for by Mr. Nana, and we got the news from our mother that in a week we would be leaving for Liberia, and that she would follow later. Mr. Nana also gave his mother enough money for food for us and money for school to get us registered as soon as we arrived. I did not want to leave, but my mother said Prikar would be moving and there would be no one to help her look after us. The week came faster than I could have imagined, and it was time for us to leave for Liberia.

The night before our trip, Mr. Nana's mother spent the night over, so we were up early to get ready for our trip and be on time so that we did not miss the bus to Liberia. My mother lied to my sister Yahgahbo and me, saying that she did not have enough money for Chakakuka to come along with us, but Mr. Nana had given her enough money for our trip and it was enough for us three to leave. What we did not know is that Chakakuka had always been her favourite and she wanted him to stay instead of us. The morning came and we hugged everyone goodbye, including Chakakuka because he wasn't leaving with us. I cried harder when it was time for the bus to leave from the Liberian refugee camp. My mother was crying when she waved to us, but she needed help and I could understand, but Yahgahbo and I were leaving with a woman we barely knew. She was a very nice older woman who loved kids very much and I knew she would love us, too.

# CHAPTER 15

# LIBERIA: THE LAND THAT FRIGHTENS US BUT A PLACE CALLED HOME

As we left for Liberia, we passed the Buduburam village and other villages along the way. The trip seemed even longer without my mother. As the bus travelled, we spent most of our time taking washroom breaks, sleeping, and eating. Mr. Nana's mother was a very nice woman and also very encouraging. She kept reminding us that we should not worry much, because our mother would be home soon to take care of us. I knew it would be a while before that happened, though. We were sad all through the trip, but as kids, we were quick to adjust to situations and to our environments, so we were adjusting to the fact that we were going to live with Mr. Nana's mother.

After almost two days on the road, we finally reached Liberia, and the place looked a bit strange but we could still remember some places. Mr. Nana's mother stayed at a place in Liberia called New Kru Town, which was known for its bad reputation as a rough place, but that was not the problem. The problem was that Mr. Nana's mother had a family member living in the house who was known for molesting little kids and even sexually abusing them.

So, Mr. Nana's sister wasn't so happy with the fact her mother brought us to the house to stay, because she knew the house wasn't a safe place. Mr. Nana's mother was always watching us to make sure nothing happened to us, but her daughter suggested that Mr. Nana's mother send us to one of our relatives to live, because if something ever happened to us our mother wouldn't forgive her, and she didn't want the good her mother was trying to do for my mother to turn into bad.

Therefore, when my mother phoned after a few days of Mr. Nana's mother thinking about it, she discussed with my mother the situation, and my mother suggested it would be a good idea for her to let us stay with her mother Stuciah in Shayon Town. Mr. Nana's mother took us there the day after their discussion, and though she did not want to leave us, she did not have much choice. My grandmother Stuciah was very happy to see us. Mr. Nana's mother explained the situation and gave my grandmother Stuciah our clothes and money for food and school.

We started to adjust, but my grandmother Stuciah needed extra help taking care of us. She had us register at a school called St. Edward Catholic School, and the principal, Mr. Alexander, knew my grandmother because he used to be an ex-boyfriend of my mother's when they were young. He was happy to see us and accepted us at the school.

Just when I started adjusting to the school, there was a problem. The school had a rule that said it was a must that every student salute the country's national flag and sing the national anthem, and with me being an unbaptized publisher at the Kingdom Hall of Jehovah's Witnesses, it's against my faith to salute the flag or pledge my allegiance to it. My allegiance belongs to Jehovah God, and Him alone. Each morning, I would hide behind a student in front of me so that I was not caught not saluting the flag while standing in line for devotion.

I was fitting in and starting to make some new friends at school, but all of it wasn't going to last for long, because the word went around that some students were refusing to salute the national flag, so Mr. Alexander and another teacher went from class to class making sure that students were saluting the flag, and the students who were refusing were pulled out of class and sent home. I knew it would be just few minutes before it was my turn.

Before they came, I wanted to ask if I could be excused to use the washroom, but the teacher said no one was allowed to leave the class until the inspections were done, so there, and then I knew I was in for some big trouble. Mr. Alexander and the other teacher entered the classroom for inspection and told us to salute the flag. While everyone was saluting the flag, I refused to put my hands up and pledge my allegiance.

I was caught and sent to Mr. Alexander's office. While I was waiting for Mr. Alexander to return, there were so many things I was thinking about, and one was how I was going to tell my grandmother Stuciah that I was being kicked out of school for not saluting the flag.

Mr. Alexander returned to his office and told me that the law making every student salute the flag was out of his hands and there was not much he could do about it. He said the only way the school was going to allow me to stay was if I saluted the flag. I said I would not and cannot because it is against my religious beliefs, and at that, Mr. Alexander had no choice but to send me away from the school.

When I got home, I told my grandmother Stuciah, and she was very upset about the school sending me home for not saluting the flag, so she promised me that the next morning she would follow me to talk some sense into their heads. The next morning came and we both went to the school together so my grandmother Stuciah could talk to the supervisors, but they refused to let me back in unless I saluted the country's national flag, which I still refused to do.

My grandmother Stuciah asked the school for a refund of my school tuition so that she can register me into another school, but the school said they would not be returning any tuition fees since that was the school's policy. My grandmother Stuciah, though, being mad, had no choice but to accept it and take me home. Every morning, I would watch as Yahgahbo would go to school in the morning and return in the afternoon while I stayed home doing nothing much but helping around the house with some housework.

One day my Grand-aunty Kombaah came to visit her mother Caba, who is my great-grandmother, and saw that I was not in school. When she asked my grandmother Stuciah, my grandmother told her what happened. After they both discussed it, she told my grandmother Stuciah that since I was not in school now, she would like me to come and stay at her place until my mother returned, and maybe she could look for a school closer to where she lived. My grandmother Stuciah didn't have the money to re-register me into another school and agreed to let me follow my Grand-aunty Kombaah.

I would stay with her until my mother returned, so Grand-aunty Kombaah told me that she would go home and discuss it with her husband, Grand-uncle Edward, and then come and pick me up on the weekend. When Yahgahbo and Sarafina came home from school and learned that I would be leaving with my Grand-aunty Kombaah, they weren't happy about it, so they said that when my Grand-aunty Kombaah came to get me, they would tell her that they would all like to come along with us.

When they said that, I got a bit worried because I did not want my Grand-aunty Kombaah changing her mind about letting me stay at her place. The weekend came and I just could not wait for my Grand-aunty Kombaah to pick me up; I had my things all packed and ready to go. When Grand-aunty Kombaah came to get me, Yahgahbo and my Aunty Sarafina were crying and wanting to come with us.

Grand-aunty Kombaah told them that she had already asked Grand-uncle Edward if I could stay there for a while and he had already agreed, so that is why she came to pick me up, plus they were all in school and I was home doing nothing. When it came time to leave, Yahgahbo and Sarafina stood there looking sad, and I was feeling bad, too, but at the same time very much excited to be spending time with my Grand-aunty Kombaah and family.

We finally got to my Grand-aunty Kombaah's house. Her family was out, except for a family member from her husband's side who lived with them. Her name was Maymay. Grand-aunty Kombaah told me that I would be sharing a room with Maymay and to take my bags into her room. I did not mind because I liked Maymay very much; she had always been very nice to me and always looked out for me when I was around.

After, I went into the kitchen to help Maymay with the cooking. Later on, Grand-aunty Kombaah's kids came home. She had a girl named Xenna and a boy named Edward, who was named after his father. Xenna seemed happy to see me, but she was also concerned about how long I would be staying at their house and when would my mother return to get me.

Xenna was not a big fan of mine, and warned me not to go into her room without her approval. Maymay even warned me to stay away from Xenna, because if Xenna complained more than once to her father, Grand-uncle Edward, he would have to ask Grand-aunty Kombaah to send me back to my grandmother Stuciah. Xenna was his princess, and he would do anything just to see her happy, but her brother Edward was very kind to me. He would want us to play with his toys, and even to go out in the yard to ride his bicycle, and he would teach me how to rollerblade.

Edward made me feel welcome and at home, and when he got home from school, he would come looking for me all the time, but Xenna would just greet me then go right to her room and chat with her friends whose parents were rich. After helping Maymay each day with housework and the cooking, we would sit and she would tell me stories. Sometimes, Maymay would even allow me to go out and play with other kids in the neighbourhood but made sure I was back before Grand-aunty Kombaah or Grand-uncle Edward came home.

When Xenna would have her friends over, she would tell me I was not allowed in her room and that her friends were not my friends. Xenna only allowed me into her room when she wanted me to do something for her, like polishing her nails or braiding her hair or helping her clean her room.

Even when she asked me to clean her room, she would usually warn me not to touch anything, which I did not even intend to do. After about a month of living there, Grand-uncle Edward started to complain about me staying there and would argue most evenings with Grand-aunty Kombaah about her allowing me to stay over and how it was cutting into their family budget. I could hear Grand-aunty Kombaah saying to him, "How much money are we spending on her and how much food do you think she's eating?"

He couldn't answer, and he also brought up the topic about my Grand-aunty Kombaah wanting to register me in school and how it was going to cost money they didn't have, and that he was not going to allow me to go to school because I was not their responsibility.

I remember the morning that Grand-aunty Kombaah wanted me to come with her to town. I always loved riding with her in her car. For some reason, I have always felt like her other daughter because that is how she made me feel just being around her, because she always loved and cared for me.

While riding with her that morning, Grand-aunty Kombaah told me she had something that she wanted to tell me. I was a bit worried at first and thought that she was going to tell me that she would like to return me to my grandmother Stuciah's house, but that was not what was on her mind. She said to me that she knew she had promised to get me registered in school because she did not like the fact that I was at home doing nothing, and that was the very reason she brought me from my grandmother Stuciah's house.

She said to me that Grand-uncle Edward was refusing to let that happen, and she did not want to upset him too much since he wouldn't change his mind about allowing me to stay at their house until my mother returned.

I told my Grand-aunty Kombaah that I understood and promised to be on my best behaviour so that Grand-uncle Edward did not get mad and send me away. That evening when we returned, I went right into the kitchen and helped Maymay get dinner ready for Grand-aunty Kombaah and her family, and when we were done, we both ate together out of a big bowl. Grand-aunty Kombaah noticed I was not eating with them at the table, and when she asked me about it, I told her it was because I liked eating with Maymay, so Grand-aunty Kombaah was OK with that.

That evening after Maymay and I finished all of the housework, it was very late in the evening, almost midnight. Maymay and I always took a shower together as big sister and little sister, but that night something strange happened, which made me careful from then on. While Maymay and I were in the shower, there was a knock on the washroom door from Grand-uncle Edward. I was very surprised and didn't understand what it was he wanted at that time of the night.

Maymay knew what it was he wanted, but she did not say, all she told me was that I should not say anything and that she would deal with him. So Maymay responded, saying that we were taking a shower, but Grand-uncle Edward kept insisting he needed me to come and do something for him. Maymay screamed from the washroom, saying that I was busy having my shower. So he left, but before he could leave, he said that after my shower he still wanted to see me, because he had something that he wanted me to do for him.

At the time Xenna had travelled to the United States of America, her room was empty, and for some reason Grand-uncle Edward decided not to sleep in the same bedroom as my Grand-aunty Kombaah but rather sleep in Xenna's room, which was right next to Maymay's bedroom.

While Maymay and I were in the shower, Maymay told me that we should hurry up and shower before Grand-uncle Edward returned. We hurried up and went into Maymay's room, put on our nightgowns, lay in bed, and we said our prayers. But before prayers were over there was a knock on the door and we knew it was Grand-uncle Edward. We didn't answer him, we just continued with our prayers, but the knock kept coming nonstop.

After our prayers were over, Maymay screamed at him, asking him what he wanted. He kept requesting me, but Maymay told him that I was fast asleep. He said it was a lie and kept on knocking on the door. Maymay told me that I should not be afraid, that no matter what he does, she was not going to open the door for him, and she was not going to send me out to get him whatever it was that he was requesting.

I was scared that if I didn't obey Grand-uncle Edward, I would get sent back to my grandmother Stuciah's place, which I didn't mind much, but I loved spending time with my Grand-aunty Kombaah. Maymay told me that I would not be going anywhere, and I was not sure what to do but I did just as Maymay told me. The next morning came, and when I saw Grand-uncle Edward during breakfast hour, I greeted him but he did not respond; he just walked past me and went to have his breakfast.

Grand-uncle Edward always ate a Liberian dish called dry rice for his breakfast, but it is cooked in such a delicious way that most times I wouldn't eat cereal and milk, I would just wait until he was done eating then eat whatever was left. That morning, before Grand-uncle Edward could leave the house, he called me and gave me a warning, saying that Maymay is not the owner of his house and that the next time he called me I had better make sure to come.

He also complained to my Grand-aunty Kombaah that I did not respect him when he called me, that I had ignored him the night before. So, when Grand-aunty Kombaah asked me later on if it was true, Maymay defended me, saying that we had already gone to bed and were fast asleep when Grand-uncle Edward was requesting me. My Grand-aunty Kombaah said that I should just be careful not to disrespect my Grand-uncle Edward intentionally. I said OK, and after my Grand-aunty Kombaah left for town, Maymay told me to not be afraid and to tell her anything and everything that anyone tried to do to me.

At first, I did not get what she was trying to tell me, but I would find out later. After everything that happened, Grand-uncle Edward no longer requested Maymay to serve him; I was the one he was requesting for everything. If Grand-uncle Edward needed wine, he would call me to get it. If he needed food, he would call me to get it. Everything he needed, I was the one getting it for him, and it was very awkward that he would walk around the house with just his underpants on, and sometimes there would be holes in them, making them see-through.

I was usually embarrassed, but Grand-uncle Edward couldn't care less. Sometimes he would be lying in his daughter Xenna's room and would ask me to come and massage his feet while he lay there in just his underwear. I was very nervous, but still had to do what Grand-uncle Edward asked me to do. One day, a friend and a male member from his family came to visit him, and I overheard them say, "Who's that young little thing you got staying with you?"

He replied to them, saying, "She's the grandniece to my wife Kombaah," and started to explain who-only-knows-what, because I wasn't around to hear everything, but the little I heard, I told Maymay, and she said, "They better not bring no foolishness around you, because I am going to set them straight."

One of the guys visiting called me and said that he wanted me to get him a drink from inside the house. When I returned, he was sitting alone and said he wanted to ask me something and that I should come closer. I did, and he asked if I could keep a secret. I did not answer, I just stood there listening to what he had to say. He told me that he would like it if I could be his little girlfriend and to keep it a secret and not tell anyone. He also said that if I told anyone, they would not believe me because he was a cousin to Grand-uncle Edward and that no one was going to believe a little girl like me.

I asked if I could be excused, and when I got into the house, I went straight into the kitchen to Maymay and told her what the guy said, and she believed me and told me to wait for her in the kitchen. Maymay went outside to that guy and gave him a piece of her mind, and told him that if she ever saw him come close to me, she would deal with him herself. Maymay came back into the kitchen and told me that if they need anything outside, she would go get it for them.

So not long after, Grand-uncle Edward went outside with the other man. Apparently they were both inside having some kind of meeting. He called me to get them drinks, but Maymay responded saying that she had me busy in the kitchen helping her cook and that she would bring them whatever it was that they needed. The cousin of Grand-uncle Edward who was interested in me started to ask him questions about me, like where I was from.

The kitchen wasn't far from where they sat, and they were talking pretty loudly. I could just hear as Grand-uncle Edward explained about me, then the guy said to him that I seemed frisky. Grand-uncle Edward said that he was not going to allow my friskiness in his house. They left very late. At that time, Maymay and I were getting the kitchen cleaned up so we could get ready for bed.

After all the guests had left and Grand-uncle Edward was very drunk, but by that time Maymay and I had cleaned up the kitchen, taken our shower, and got into bed. We heard Grand-uncle Edward screaming our names, which we ignored and pretended to be fast asleep. The next morning when we woke, Grand-uncle Edward had gotten ready for work and was not in the mood to request anything from us.

He ate his breakfast, and usually he would tell Maymay what he wanted to eat later before he left for work, but that day he did not say a word, he just left. So Maymay said she would cook whatever we were in the mood to eat that day. She cooked cassava gravy and we enjoyed it. Usually when we were done early, we would sit down and she would tell me about her childhood. I would laugh at the funny ones, and I would just feel sorry for her over the sad ones.

She said Xenna and little Edward had no respect for her, and she did not really care much about them, she just did her work around the house and minded her business as much as possible. When little Edward would come home from school, he would go outside to do his homework, and because I wasn't in school I would sometimes take his school books after he was done studying and I would read them over, but when Grand-uncle Edward saw me reading Edward's books, he would tell me that I should stop making noise and that I didn't know how to read. At the time, I did not know how to read quietly, so when I read I would read aloud.

Apparently, Grand-uncle Edward didn't like that I was using Edward's books to read, so he complained to my Grand-aunty Kombaah, and she told me that if I needed books to read she would get me some. A few days later, Grand-aunty Kombaah told Maymay and me that we should make sure the house was clean because she was expecting a visitor from America. Xenna would be returning from America as well, and she needed her room really clean, because she would like to redecorate it and put in new wallpaper.

Me, with my silly self, did not know what wallpaper was, but I soon found out. Xenna had already warned me before travelling that if I was ever to clean her room not to touch anything in it, because everything belonged to her. So, as I was assigned to clean Xenna's room for her return from America, I had to keep reminding myself not to touch anything but just clean and get out.

Now that day while cleaning Xenna's room, I came across a book called *The Babysitter's Club*. I stopped what I was doing and started to read it a little bit and found it very interesting, so I put it aside to read later when I was done cleaning her room, then I would read it in my own time. After I was done, I took the book into the kitchen with me, and as Maymay cooked I began reading it.

Maymay asked me where I got the book, and I told her Xenna's bedroom. She told me that I was looking for trouble, because Xenna warned me never to touch anything in her room, but I needed something to keep my mind busy and found the book interesting. Though I still helped Maymay with work around the house, when I was not busy I found time to read, and in less than a week I was back into Xenna's room searching for other books of the *Babysitters' Club*. In her room, I found lots more but would only borrow one at a time.

The day came when Xenna and their guest finally arrived from America, and everyone was excited to see them; there was lots of food cooked and other family and guests came over to visit, too. However, Xenna was kind of excited to see me at their house still, but she was concerned as to why my mother had not returned to get me. The guest from America did not stay too long at the house; they had other places to visit. After the guest left and things were back to normal in the house, Xenna noticed me reading one of her *Babysitter's Club* books.

She didn't like the idea that I disobeyed her orders, but when she learned how many of her books I had read, she told me that I could only read the ones she had already read, which I agreed to and so she gave me more of her old books and I was very happy to have something interesting to occupy my time with. So, I kept myself busy reading when I was not busy helping Maymay in the kitchen and around the house. I remember one day: Grand-uncle Edward came home and saw me reading, and said to me, "Do you understand anything from that book, or are you just looking at the writing?"

I just continued my reading and let no one distract me from learning. Sometimes when I felt sad and missed my family, I would go outside and start to sing songs from the Kingdom Hall of Jehovah's Witnesses songbook to give me hope that one day everything was going to be OK, but Grand-uncle Edward would come outside and say to me, "Stop making noise, saying you can sing." Then he would call out to Xenna and say, "Come here, come sing for me with your lovely voice." It did get to me a bit, but all that helped me to be strong and continue to believe in myself. Sometimes Grand-aunty Kombaah would sit outside with her family and I would go into Maymay's room and cry, wishing that one day my family and I would be together like this.

On Sunday, Grand-aunty Kombaah would take me to the meeting at the Kingdom Hall of Jehovah's Witnesses. On our way we would talk, and she would ask me questions and tell me not to pay too much attention to Grand-uncle Edward's behaviour. She would tell me that he was just a miserable man who does not like very many people, and that one day his selfish ways would catch up with him and we would both laugh.

After meetings, when Grand-aunty Kombaah took her family out, she would take me along with her. In some sense, she was the mother I wished I had, and that is why she has always been my favourite Grand-aunty, whom I love just as much as my very own mother.

Coming along, Grand-uncle Edward was not happy, but as Grand-aunty Kombaah had said to not pay him any attention, I didn't. I did not look into his face; I went along and had fun. Sometimes, though, when they were going out I got to stay home. For example, when they would go to visit Grand-uncle Edward's brother Bardi. I did not mind staying home, because it allowed me to keep up with my book reading. Xenna was not close to me; she kept enough distance from me because she felt we were not on the same level of life.

When her friends would come to visit her and I would sit with them, she would tell me that her friends were not my friends and that I should go and make friends out there. When her friends came and asked for her, I just told them she was in her room, and they went in to see her. Sometimes I heard them ask her why she didn't like me very much, and I would hear her tell them that I was very annoying and how she couldn't stand me and how she couldn't wait until I left.

When I told Maymay what Xenna said about me, Maymay would tell me, "Well, that is why you need to just stay in your space and leave her alone," but all I wanted was to connect with her and get to know her, but that wasn't possible because my family no longer had money, so I was no longer in the same class as her. I remember one day, when Xenna's friends from her school came over to visit. Apparently, they did not live far from us, so at the end of their visit she decided to walk with her friends. I begged Xenna to let me come along and she said no, but I still insisted I was going to go anyway.

I waited for them to walk a bit ahead and then I started to follow them, and when Xenna's friends noticed that I was following them, they told her and she stopped and told me to return home, but I told her I wasn't following her, that I was just going for a walk.

She told her friends that they should walk slower so that I would catch up with them, and then she would discipline me. Xenna waited until I came closer, and then she started to chase me, and when she caught up with me, she beat me and said that she told me to return home and I had refused. I was crying but I insisted on following them, so she told her friends that they should walk faster so that I could not catch up with them. After trying, I could not find them, so I decided to return home.

On my way home, there was a compound just opposite from where Grand-aunty Kombaah lived, and the kids in the compound were very friendly. They asked me for my name and introduced themselves to me; they also told me that I could visit them whenever I wasn't busy. They said to me that I was much friendlier than my cousin Xenna, because she had never greeted or befriended them.

When I got home, I told Maymay about the new friends I'd made, and she told me it was OK for me to go there and visit them as long as no one was home, but to make sure I returned before anyone got home. Since I had new friends who lived next door now, I made sure to help Maymay with everything in the house, like the cleaning and cooking first, then I went to play. I did memorize the sound of Grand-aunty Kombaah's car, so whenever I was playing and I heard her car coming from a distance, I would run home and pretend I had been home all day.

This went on for a while, but my Grand-aunty Kombaah learned that I was not staying in the yard to play. How did she find out? It was because of my cousin Xenna, who was at home one day and wanted me to polish her toes, but I wasn't in the yard. When she asked Maymay if she had sent me to buy something, Maymay told her that I was just next door playing with the other kids in their yard.

Xenna sent the security at the gate to go and get me. The security came and told me that I was requested at the house, and when I came along, Xenna asked me what I was doing befriending the kids next door. I told her it was because I needed friends to play with. When Grand-aunty Kombaah and Grand-uncle Edward came home, Xenna told them, and they told me that they needed me to stay in the compound for my own safety. Grand-uncle Edward told the security not to let me leave the yard to go out to play.

Grand-aunty Kombaah took food to her mother Caba every month and made sure that her place was clean, because she is blind and cannot see to clean her own place. On this day, Grand-aunty Kombaah was going over to see my great-grandmother Caba to take over some food and to make sure that her place was clean; she took Xenna and me along with her so we could visit with the family.

Yahgahbo and Sarafina had been playing in the yard and were looking dirty from playing, so when we got there I was very happy to see everyone, including my grandmother Stuciah. When I tried to go to Sarafina and Yahgahbo to greet them and chat with them, they gave me attitude and said that because I was now living with Grand-aunty Kombaah that I was starting to think that I was better than they were, but that wasn't the way I felt.

Xenna only came down from the car to greet her grandmother Caba and my grandmother Stuciah, who is Xenna's aunty, and to help her mother with a bit of cleaning, and then went back to sit in the car. Xenna was not very proud of where her grandmother Caba and Aunty Stuciah were staying, and her attitude to the environment told it all. It was almost time for us to leave, so Grand-aunty Kombaah went and sat with her sister Stuciah.

They talked for a bit and laughed about certain things and had a bit to eat with me, and before she could leave she gave her sister Stuciah some money to help her out and suggested that their mother needed more attention in her care, and my grandmother promised to have that taken care of. My great-grandmother can at times be very mouthy and that makes it frustrating for my grandmother Stuciah to give her the kind of care she needs. We said goodbye and off we went, but on our way back I was not very talkative, so Grand-aunty Kombaah noticed that I was not myself.

She then asked me what the problem was, and when I explained Sarafina and Yahgahbo's behaviour toward me, she told me not to pay too much attention to that and that sometimes you cannot change the way people behave to you, but you can change the way you react to them. We drove back to where my Grand-aunty Kombaah lived, but on our way there she had to run some errands and pick some things up for the house, like food. On the road there were women selling things wholesale, like fish and other good stuff.

My Grand-aunty Kombaah would get some to take home and that would mean Maymay and I were going to be busy all night in the kitchen trying to package everything. We finally got to the house, unloaded the things from the car, and took them into the house for cleaning and packaging, while Xenna went into her room to listen to her Walkman and read her book and relax as Maymay prepared the table for them to have dinner.

Maymay asked me about my visit; I told her about Sarafina and Yahgahbo's attitude toward me, and she told me to not pay them any attention. That evening, after serving dinner, Maymay and I had a lot to do putting the food away and making sure the kitchen stayed clean for the next day.

Xenna was now back from her visit, but Grand-uncle Edward would still send me to get stuff for him and he would usually just walk around the house in torn-up underpants. Sometimes he would not sleep in the same room with my Grand-aunty Kombaah, he would sleep in his son Edward's bedroom, and sometimes when he sent me for something, I would get nervous because he would be lying in his son's bedroom with just underpants on watching a movie.

Maymay would sometimes tell him to send Xenna for stuff because I was busy helping her in the kitchen. When he called Xenna, she would complain about being very busy and wished not to be disturbed, and then he would promise to buy her something. That was the only way she would get up and get him what he wanted. Maymay would sometimes say to me, "Look, their kids are so disrespectful to their parents but they spoil them."

I remember one day I was outside missing my family, so I started to sing a song from the songbook of the Jehovah's Witnesses just to cheer myself up when Grand-uncle Edward came and told me that I was making too much noise and that my voice sounded horrible. At that, he called to his daughter Xenna to come out and sing for him, and said that she had such a lovely voice. Even though I was little, I did not believe a word he said about my singing being bad, I just knew he was trying to make me feel bad and unimportant.

I closed my songbook, and as I was going into the house, Grand-aunty Kombaah came outside and told him that was not the way to speak to a child. When Maymay asked me what happened, I explained it to her. She told me, "Well, I told you to mind your business in this house and keep to yourself, but you like putting yourself in a position to make yourself feel bad. This is not your parents' house; these kids will always come first and you last, so stop trying so hard to fit in."

One day, one of Xenna's family members came to visit. His name was Aaron and he was very good looking, and though I didn't know how old he was, he was probably around Maymay's age, twenty-five, or just a little bit younger. I started to have feelings for him, as in having a crush on him, and he found it strange that this little girl liked him and would joke around with him when he came. I would joke with him, calling him "little cat," and he would joke back and respond with "little rat."

Maymay didn't like the idea, and told me to stop joking with this guy because we were not of the same age, but each time he would come around my heart would just leap with so much joy. But Maymay kept a watchful eye on me. Maymay always cared for me like a big sister would care for her little sister. Sometimes Xenna's other cousins, the ones I knew for sure were their cousins—their Uncle Bardi's kids, Demakana and Toko—would come for visit, and we would all play in the yard together and have so much fun.

When Demakana and Toko would ask if I could come and spend time with them, Xenna would say no, and then Grand-aunty Kombaah would tell them maybe another time, just so I didn't feel all that bad. One day while Grand-aunty Kombaah was away at work, my grandmother sent someone to Grand-aunty Kombaah's house to let us know that my mother had returned and wished to see me, and that when Grand-aunty Kombaah came home, to let her know to bring me back to my grandmother Stuciah's house.

I was very happy to hear the news, but at the same time very sad that I was going to miss my Grand-aunty Kombaah, Maymay, and my cousin Edward, but as for Xenna, I wasn't sure if I was going to miss her, because all the time I was there she didn't take the time to connect with me and there were no emotional attachments between us.

# CHAPTER 16

# MY MOTHER DEBORAH'S RETURN FROM GHANA: THE GOOD NEWS

The rest of that day before my Grand-aunty Kombaah returned from work to hear the news, Maymay was unhappy because she was going to miss me lots—I was her only friend in the house. I respected her like her younger sister, and we talked about almost everything. Maymay was sad, and I was very sad as well. When Grand-aunty Kombaah returned from work and got the message, she was in tears the rest of the day and did not come out for dinner.

She just stayed in her room and asked Maymay to make soup for her, saying that she was not feeling well, but I knew it was because I was leaving and there was not much she could do because my mother was the one requesting me. The next day, Grand-aunty Kombaah did not go into work; she told me that she would go over to my grandmother Stuciah's house to see my mother and then she would ask my mother when she would like me to return home.

Grand-aunty Kombaah got ready to go but didn't have much of an appetite for breakfast, so she just left and told me she would be back. When she got to my grandmother's house, my mother had returned with Chakakuka and everyone was there to see her.

My Grand-aunty Kombaah asked if she could return me on the weekend, that way I would get to spend a little bit more time at her house, and my mother agreed. It was almost time for the weekend, and as I got ready to return, Maymay was sad and so was my Grand-aunty Kombaah and cousin Edward. His dad, Grand-uncle Edward, said the house was going to be so quiet when I was gone, and I was surprised to see that it seemed as though he was also going to miss me, because he mostly behaved as if he did not want me around.

Xenna, on the other hand, started to be nice to me and was giving me some of her stuff that she did not want any more so that I could take it home with me. The ones I really felt deep emotion for were my Grand-aunty Kombaah, Cousin Edward, and Maymay, and leaving was really hurting me. I was trying to be strong, but the emotions I felt kept getting real and I started to cry. I missed my own family, but I missed what some would call a perfect family, the one where there is a mom and dad in the house who looked after everything and made sure that the kids were taken care of.

Now, I am not saying that my Grand-aunty Kombaah's family was prefect, because most times Grand-uncle Edward did not sleep in the same room as my Grand-aunty Kombaah. What I am trying to say is that my Grand-aunty Kombaah made her family seem perfect because she didn't want to end up like the rest of her family, being a single mother with no father around, and because of that she took a lot of mess from Grand-uncle Edward, like when he cheated and beat her up.

When she was out, she always pretended that her home and relationship were all good, but yet she was hurting lots inside and I felt sorry for her. The weekend came and it was time for me to go to my grandmother Stuciah's house to see my mother. That morning, I said my goodbyes to everyone and off I went.

As we were driving to my grandmother Stuciah's house, my Grand-aunty Kombaah told me that I was welcome to go and visit her whenever I wanted to, and to even come and spend some time, but I would need to ask my mother first. When we arrived at my grandmother Stuciah's house, everyone was having a good time as though they were having a party.

I guess everyone was just excited to see my mother, because the house was full of other relatives who came to see her. My mother was cooking a big pot of food and my grandmother Stuciah had sent for some cold beer and there were soft drinks for the kids in the house. Adjusting from my newfound life to living at my grandmother Stuciah's house again was going to take me some time, but it happened quickly by just playing outside with all my old friends again.

Sarafina, Yahgahbo, and Chakakuka were very happy to see me, and I was happy to see them as well, but they sometimes would look at me as though I was behaving differently. The reason for that was that I had become accustomed to other things, such as spending some time reading and keeping myself clean and not getting myself all dirty when I went out to play. My Grand-aunty Kombaah stayed for a while, but then she had to leave. But before she left, she sent for me, but at my grandmother Stuciah's place, if you call one person everyone came, because they knew you were probably going to give that person money and they all wanted their share.

So, when my Grand-aunty Kombaah sent for me, Sarafina, Chakakuka, and Yahgahbo all came running. For sure she was calling me to give me some money to buy things if I needed them, but because everyone came, she had to share whatever she wanted to give me with them as well, and I didn't mind.

I gave my Grand-aunty Kombaah a very big hug, and with tears in my eyes I said my goodbyes. By the time she left my mood was not so great, but it went back to being normal in no time. At the end of the day when everything calmed down, my mother asked me about my stay, and she told me about her stay after we left her in Ghana and almost all the things that happened while we were away.

My mother shared a room with my Aunty Wawanibo, while we all slept outside on the floor in the kitchen/sitting area because there was not enough space in my grandmother Stuciah's house. The place had two bedrooms, a sitting area that was also used for a kitchen, and a little space outside that we used for a shower. My Aunty Peyeeh started building her own house in the space my grandmother Stuciah had given her.

Sometimes when she was going over to spend time with her Lebanese man, she would give her keys to her adopted daughter Sedahmar, and tell her that we could sleep over, too, if we wanted. My grandmother Stuciah decided that my brother would still sleep in the kitchen area with my other uncles, and we as girls would sleep in Aunty Peyeeh's place. My mother and my aunties would go out to the club and have fun. They would come home late from their outing and stay up all night laughing and chatting.

My mother moved into town to one of her friend's places, and I'm not sure how the story went, but she would occasionally come to see us. Something happened between my mother and her sister, and her mother and my mother said to us that we were not to eat any food that my grandmother Stuciah or my aunties cooked. My mother started to pay some woman who had a local restaurant to cook food for us to eat every day, so each day when the woman cooked, she would send someone to my grandmother Stuciah's house to get us so we could go and eat.

Sometimes when my Aunty Peyeeh or grandmother Stuciah would cook, they would still give us food to eat and tell us not to tell our mother. It wasn't long before my mother found an apartment for rent in Mamba Point, but she said the apartment wasn't yet furnished and that she would only be taking Chakakuka to stay with her for a while until she could get the place furnished, because she needed a male figure in her apartment so no one would steal from her.

She said that once her apartment was furnished, she would come and get Yahgahbo and me so that we could go and live with her, but I didn't know that my mother had started dating a white guy who worked at the American embassy; I'm not sure what position he had there, but it was a pretty good one because he used to give my mother a lot of money. She told the man that she only had one child, Chakakuka, and the man only knew of him.

My mother would visit Yahgahbo and me once a month at my grandmother Stuciah's house just to drop off enough food to manage us for the month, and when she came she wouldn't stay too long before she left again. Whenever I asked her when we would be able to go and live with her, she would find all the excuses in the world to give us. I started to get concerned. Sometimes, she would even bring Chakakuka along with her to visit us and he would start to behave as if he was better than us, and would even talk about the things our mother did for him and how good life was.

I started to get mad, and sometimes when my mother would come to bring us our monthly supplies I would refuse to greet her until she threatened that if I did not show up to greet her she would beat me badly. Sometimes, I would hear her and my grandmother arguing in the room.

Their arguments weren't clear, but apparently my grandmother Stuciah would be telling her that her behaviour towards us wasn't fair and that she would need to take us to live with her at Mamba Point, and my mother would respond by saying that she wasn't ready yet.

So, one day, my grandmother Stuciah, who'd had enough of my mother's nonsense, told me that my mother didn't love us, that she only loved Chakakuka and that is why she lied to the white man and told him that she only had one child, and that was the reason she only had Chakakuka living with her at her Mamba Point apartment. This made me upset, and I wondered how my mother could have done this to us.

I would just sit by myself and cry, knowing that my mother disowned us and did not want any connection to us and had just left us at my grandmother's house while she and Chakakuka had their prefect life as mother and son. The day came when my mother was to bring our regular monthly supplies, and I just could not wait to look into her eyes and ask her if everything my grandmother said was true. I was playing outside with my friends when my mother arrived in a taxi with our food supplies.

I was excited to see her, because it has been a month, but the problem was still on my mind, and had me wondering how my mother could behave like she loved us so much but then say we were not her daughters and that Chakakuka was her only child. That day, she noticed that I wasn't in such a good mood, and when she asked what was wrong I said nothing was wrong. She insisted that I stand right in front of her and tell her what was troubling me.

In tears, I told her exactly what my grandmother Stuciah had told me and then I ran off. Later, I came around and my grandmother Stuciah and my mother were having a heated argument about why she told me, and I heard my grandmother Stuciah telling my mother that as a mother she shouldn't choose between children because that can create jealousy and hate when kids start to grow up.

My mother was so mad at the truth my grandmother Stuciah was telling her that she told us to pack our things, and that we were no longer going to stay at my grandmother Stuciah's, because she claimed that her mother was trying to turn us against her and make us feel that we were unwanted. We packed our things and my mother sent for a taxi so she could take us back to her place at Mamba Point.

I felt sad, because I would miss hanging out with my grandmother Stuciah, helping her sew, cooking together, staying up late at night listening to her many beautiful stories and drinking beer together, and being able to talk about anything. My mother did not know that my grandmother had been giving us beer to drink, because if she did it would have been a big fight between them.

My Aunty Sarafina was crying to see us leave, and we in turn were crying because we were going to miss the time we spent together connecting and playing. My mother told Yahgahbo and me that when we got to the apartment in Mamba Point there were some things she would like to talk to us about. As we drove excitedly to see our new place, we could not stop wondering what it was she wanted to talk to us about. As the taxi drove into the Mamba Point area, the place looked different from where my grandmother Stuciah lived and the area was a lot nicer.

The taxi came to a stop, we were finally there, and some people in the area stood and watched to see who was moving in or visiting. My mother sent someone to call Chakakuka to come downstairs to help carry our bags into the apartment. My mother's apartment was only two bedrooms, meaning that we would be sharing a bedroom with Chakakuka, and for us that was going to be a bit challenging because he did not like sharing very much.

He liked to be in control, and he feels everything is his because he is the only boy. Well, after we were all settled in and had something to eat, our mother said that she would like to talk to the three of us about how things were going to run around the house. First, she had to explain about what my grandmother Stuciah said about her saying we were not her daughters and about Chakakuka being her only child.

As she sat explaining there were tears in her eyes. Now, I was not sure that those tears were because she was truly sorry or because she was just ashamed, but I was willing to know the truth about why she would do a thing like that. She told us how she had met this white man and she was afraid of losing him, so she lied to him, saying that she only had one child. Chakakuka got introduced to him, and he only knew Chakakuka, but now she would have to tell him about us because sometimes he does come over to her apartment to visit. But until she could introduce us, we should call her Dee instead of Mama.

Just hearing my mother say that hurt even more, and it really had me thinking how right my grandmother Stuciah was and how I wished I was not even living with my mother. She went on explaining how, when she's not around, Chakakuka would be in charge of everything, including the keys to the house and the cupboard and fridge because they had locks on them as well.

She said we were to listen to Chakakuka's instructions because he was the oldest, he was in charge, and that if we refused to listen to him she would discipline us when she got back. She also told me I would be responsible for the cooking of the house and making sure that Chakakuka and Yahgahbo helped me keep the house clean. After her explanation, she said it was time for us to go to bed. That night when we went to bed, it was just a queen-sized mattress on the floor. It was big enough for all of us to fit on, but Chakakuka, being so selfish, did not want to share the mattress with us.

He took the spot closest to the wall of the bedroom, and when he lay down he positioned his feet in a way where we were only given a little space to sleep, not enough for both of us. When we asked him to make space for us to sleep, he said, "I don't know why you guys had to come here, my mother and I were doing OK and I had my bed all to myself, and now I got to share it with you guys."

We then started to argue with him, saying that she wasn't just his mother, she's our mother, too, and we all had a right to stay where she lived. But hey, I can't blame him, she chose to make him her only child by denying us and claiming we were just her little sisters. She heard us all arguing in the room and came in and demanded that Chakakuka make space for us on the bed, and said that we all better fall asleep before she returned and was forced to whip us to bed. The next morning came and my mother made breakfast for us all, and we said a prayer to Jehovah God telling him thanks and asking him to guide and protect us as one family.

Later, she sent for some boys who lived in the neighbourhood that she usually sent on errands, introduced us as her kids, and told them that they were assigned to keep an eye on us for her. Later, we learned that those boys were living underneath the apartment stairs.

The place had no windows, only a door, and from the look of it, I think it was a storage space they had turned into a room. In addition, we would learn that they were always taking girls in there to have sex with them, but whatever they did, they never, ever brought foolishness around Yahgahbo and me. My mother later sent one of the boys to the market to buy some foodstuffs for her to cook, and then the other helped her with fresh water and the laundry.

After the boys returned from the market, my mother began cooking food for us to eat and I helped her. When she was done cooking and we had eaten and washed all the dirty dishes, she told us that we could go out to play and try to make some friends, but to also be aware of the kind of friends we were making. We had a Nigerian person who lived next door with his woman and their kids, and he had a daughter named Rere and two other boys and some family members living with them as well.

One of her family members was a boy named Jey-Boy, who I think had a crush on every girl he saw, and I was sure he had experience with sex. He was a friend of Chakakuka's, and Rere made friends with Yahgahbo and me. Another neighbour family was East Indian; they had a son called Chake. Below us was a guy who had lots of money; his name was Sahger and he was dating and living with a beautiful mixed-race lady called Pamala. This lady was an exact photocopy of the American actress Julia Roberts. Next to them was a family who had a mixed-race daughter named Chichi.

Chichi also became friends with us, and later we would learn that Chakakuka started dating her. Rere had a crush on Chake and Chake had a crush on Yahgahbo and Jey-Boy had a crush on me, but I didn't like him. I thought he talked too much, because the first time we ever talked to Jey-Boy he talked about every girl he ever dated or had a crush on, and for me that was a no.

We all became fast friends, but my brother, who had been there longer, knew everyone around the area, while we were just getting to know people. We went about our regular duties every day, and my mother was always gone, and Chakakuka, being in charge, started to act stupid. He would lock the entire cupboard in the kitchen, and lock the fridge as well, and when we wanted something to eat he would say to us that we would have to wait until he was ready to eat.

His attitude started to get really upsetting, and we had to think of a way to end this. Chakakuka would sometimes go outside to play, and when we asked to come along, he would say no, that our mother left him in charge of the house and whatever he says is what we would do. Yahgahbo and I would sit alone in the house and we would think of ways to end his nonsense. I now started missing the freedom I had living at my grandmother Stuciah's house. Living with my mother with Chakakuka in charge made us feel like we were in prison.

Chakakuka would only allow us to come outside when he was in the mood for us to come out to play. Once we were outside, if Chakakuka was no longer in the mood to play but we still wanted to stay out a bit, he would tell us it was time for us all to go back into the apartment. When we refused, he would threaten to lock us outside until our mother returned, then he would tell her the reason we'd been locked outside was because we refused to listen to him, and then she would beat us for not listening.

Next, he told us that if we refused to come inside when he told us to, he would not let us go play outside for a long time. Yahgahbo and I had to put a stop to this, and we had to come up with a plan really fast to make our brother show us some respect in the house. The people who owned the apartments were Lebanese and they lived in a yard next to the apartment complex.

From our back balcony, we could look right into their backyard and see everything that went on in there. Most evenings, we would go to the back balcony to watch them as they killed rabbits for dinner, and sometimes they would see us watching them. Sometimes we went to the back balcony to chat with our friends, and we would watch as Pamala made a meal for Sahger outside.

Pamala also had a sister living with her named Markadi, who was very slim with big breasts, which she was embarrassed of, and most of the time she would be indoors reading or would sometimes leave the house to go for a walk. When Pamala and her housecleaner would cook, they would make a lot of food because Sahger always had people visiting him. There was this person named Frank who worked with Sahger as his driver. He was a very good-looking person, but he was not my age; he was way older than I was, but it was funny how I had a crush on him.

Frank was always good looking and well dressed, but Chakakuka always had a tight eye on us making sure that no one tried messing with us. Each time when Pamala would come home or go out, I would stay on the front balcony and watch her. Because she was identical to Julia Roberts, I wanted so badly to be her god-daughter, so each time when she was leaving I would say goodbye to her, and when she returned I would say hello.

Because of my constant greeting, she eventually came to like me; she sent for me to help her and that was the first time I had seen inside their apartment. Their place was very nice and had everything in it, including digital television, the kind where you get to watch all of the American and international channels.

Their bedroom was every woman's dream, and she had a bedroom where her sister Markadi stayed where most of her clothes for going out were; perfume, bags, shoes, and makeup were in there as well. Their place had a "wow, oh my goodness!" kind of look. Pamala had a lot of gold jewellery that she wore on a daily basis, and when she and Sahger went out. Pamala became fond of me, and her sister Markadi liked me very much and saw me as her friend and little sister.

Sometimes when I went downstairs to Pamala's place, I would take Yahgahbo with me when she was not busy playing with her friends. Chakakuka got mad, because I was always at Pamala's apartment, so he decided to report my regular visit to our mother. She decided that if I was to be allowed to visit Pamala, she would need to meet her and have a word to make sure that I was somewhere safe. I didn't know that my mother had her own intentions.

I told Pamala about my mother's request and Pamala agreed to meet with her. The day came when Pamala and my mother were both at home. Pamala sent her sister Markadi to tell my mother that she would like both of them to meet, and that she was at home if she would like to come downstairs for a chat. My mother sent a message saying that she would be right down, but I didn't understand why my mother dressed up like she was going on a date just to go and meet with Pamala.

Later, I would learn that my mother's request to meet with Pamala was to get her closer to Pamala's lover, Sahger. My mother went downstairs to meet with Pamala, and later I could hear laughter and could tell they were having a good time.

I was mad, because Pamala was my friend not my mother's, and her getting close to Pamala kept me away, because each time I would visit my mother would say that I should leave and go play with my friends because it was a grown-up conversation. That is how Markadi and I started becoming close friends. Pamala was now always out with my mother somewhere and was never home to make dinner for Sahger.

Pamala was now always letting her housecleaner cook the food for Sahger, and when Sahger would come home she would be nowhere to be found. My mother had a mission to get Pamala to cheat on Sahger, so when Sahger found out he would leave Pamala and be available for her. Meanwhile, I kept myself busy cooking, cleaning, and playing with my newfound friends in the area.

Pamala and my mother became fast friends, and their friendship seemed as though it was unbreakable. Whenever Pamala cooked, she would send for my mother to come and eat with her, and when my mother cooked, she would return the favour. My mother also became a friend to a sister from the Kingdom Hall of Jehovah's Witnesses named Jahjah, who was married.

They had two beautiful little girls and other family members who lived in the USA. Their kids had many beautiful toys to play with, and whenever I wasn't busy at home, I would go over to visit them just to have a chance to play with their toys. Most times I would take Yahgahbo with me, and sometimes we would be there until late. Jahjah would sometimes come to visit my mother and she would visit her, too. One day when Jahjah came to visit my mother, she met Pamala at my mother's apartment.

My mother introduced them and they became friends. There was a lot in common that my mother, Deborah, and Pamala shared that Jahjah did not, so they were just regular friends with her, but not close ones. Jahjah started taking us to meetings at the Kingdom Hall of Jehovah's Witnesses along with her husband and kids, because our mother was never really home except to change and go back out, and sometimes on the weekend.

The time came for us to go back to school, and everyone was ready except me. My mother registered Chakakuka and Yahgahbo in Cathedral Catholic School and had me stay home, because she said I wasted a year of school by not saluting the flag, and she didn't have much money for me to go to school so I would need to miss another year. Though I was very upset, I did not have much of a choice; I was forced to accept and stay home as I watched Chakakuka and Yahgahbo go to school while I stayed home to clean and cook.

Whenever I was done my cleaning and cooking early, I would go downstairs to visit Markadi, or I would go over to Jahjah's place to play with her kids and their toys. I remember one weekend when my mother wasn't home and Yahgahbo and I wanted to go out to play. When we asked Chakakuka to let us go out, he said no, because he was going out to play with his friend and we had to stay indoors.

When we insisted, he said that if we went outside, he would make sure that we did not get back into the apartment. He would make sure we stayed outside until our mother returned home. He pretended he wasn't going anywhere anymore just so we would take our minds off leaving the house. When we fell asleep, he left us in the house and locked the door so there was no way of getting out of the house.

When Yahgahbo and I awoke, we were so mad and so frustrated that we came up with a plan that together we would both attack him when he walked through the door, and no matter how hard he punched us we would try not to cry or else he would think he had power over us. After he had played outside, he came inside all tired and hungry and thought he was just going to relax; well, that was not what happened.

As soon as he got inside the apartment, we asked him for the keys and said we would like to go outside to play. He said no, locked the door, and put the keys in his pocket and started to walk toward our bedroom door. There was a door in the middle of the apartment that separated the living room from the rest of the house, so his plan was to go through that door and lock it so Yahgahbo and I would be stuck in the living room with no way to go outside and no way to use the washroom or even go to the bedroom or the kitchen.

Before he could get through the door, both of us jumped him for a fight. He started to punch and slap us, but we kept fighting him for the keys. While the fight was going on, the pointy handle of the door hurt him a little. Chakakuka noticed that he was bleeding a little, took off the white shirt he was wearing and dabbed it all over with his blood, and then put it back on and said that he was going to wear it and wait for our mother to come home and see it.

Yahgahbo and I didn't even get the chance to go out to play, because after the fight happened, our mother came home from her outing. When she saw Chakakuka's bloody T-shirt, she did not ask questions, she just started screaming, "Oh my God! The two witches I brought to live with me want to kill my only son!"

Without any questions being asked, my mother whipped the life out of us for defending ourselves from the abuse and control we were enduring from Chakakuka. She gave us the beating of our lives, but I promised Chakakuka that it was not the end, that it was just the beginning of defending ourselves, so whenever he wanted to bring it on, we would be ready to fight back.

Ever since that day, Chakakuka became afraid of the team of fighting sisters, because we were determined to fight back and to not allow ourselves to get abused by him. We started to demand the keys to the cupboard and take charge of things around the house. A few months after our fight with him, Chakakuka found a new distraction for himself and we were no longer the centre of his attention.

He started dating this mixed-race girl who lived downstairs named Chichi. At first, we did not know this was going on, we were just wondering why he was not around to give us all the trouble he usually gave us. Jey-Boy, who lived next door, ran his mouth by telling us that Chakakuka had started dating Chichi, but we told him that it was a lie and that our brother had no girlfriend. Well, one day when Chakakuka didn't know we were looking over the front balcony, we saw him kissing Chichi and we were very much surprised. When he got home, we threatened to tell our mother what he did.

He begged us not to tell, so we gave him the condition that he should leave us alone to have our own freedom, and he agreed. Chichi was now allowed at our apartment to visit Chakakuka as his girlfriend, and we knew about the both of them but our mother didn't know a thing, plus she was never around to notice anything.

Yahgahbo started seeing Chake as her own lover, but I had a feeling for a man named Frank who was much older than me, and Chakakuka didn't like the idea. So for Frank to be allowed to talk to me, he became friends with Chakakuka and would sometimes buy things for him and occasionally give him money that my brother would sometimes give to Chichi for when she wanted to buy something. Because of that Chakakuka and Frank became close friends.

Frank would come and knock on the door, and Chakakuka would come to me in the kitchen and tell me that Frank was there to talk to me. I would go downstairs to meet with him, and we would just talk about normal stuff and he would ask me about my school, but I told him that I wasn't in school and that my mother said I would go to school for the next term.

Frank now knew that I was home by myself during the week a lot. When he came to pick Sahger up to take him to work but Sahger was still a little busy, Frank would ask the boys who usually helped my mother if she was around, and if they said no, Frank would come up to our apartment to greet me. We would sit on the stairs for a bit and talk, and when it was time for Sahger to leave, Frank would run down quickly to take Sahger to work.

We all had people we were interested in, and I for one was not in a rush to experience anything, plus the guy who was interested in me was much older and very afraid of getting in any kind of trouble with my mother because of me. One evening, my mother wasn't home and Chakakuka and Yahgahbo were still out playing late and Frank came up to the apartment to see me, so I came outside to greet him, and we sat on the stairs to talk.

As we talked, he kept looking at me in the eyes and I felt a little shy, a little embarrassed, a little uncomfortable, and the next thing I knew Frank started to kiss me. Not really knowing what a kiss was, I just stood there with my mouth wide open and did nothing. Before Frank kissed me, I had never been kissed by anyone unless it was my parents kissing me on the forehead. My mother and my stepdad AmiShasi usually kissed us on our foreheads when we went to bed, so when he said he wanted to kiss me, I thought he was going to kiss me on my forehead.

No, it was on my lips, and I didn't know how to react because I had never been kissed before. After kissing me, he left and told me that he would come see me the next day. I did not know what to say and what to do, but the fact that I had never been kissed and had now kissed for the very first time in my young life had me confused and thinking. Though it felt good, it was something that was different, something I had never experienced, and something nobody ever explained to me before, and I wanted to try it again.

It felt good, and I just wanted Frank around all the time. Whenever no one was around, Frank would visit me and we would talk and kiss, but that was about it. One day, Pamala's maid warned him, saying, "I just hope you know what you were doing, because that girl is a child and she's a virgin; if her mother finds out, you are dead." Frank got busy driving Sahger around, so he wasn't coming around much like he used to, but sometimes when I got really concerned I just went downstairs and asked Markadi to let him know I would like to see him.

When Frank came around, he would make sure he talked loud enough so that I could hear his voice, then I would go to the front balcony and let him know my mother was home so he wouldn't come upstairs. However, if she was not home then I would let him know from the front or the back balcony that my mother wasn't home. He would come up to say hi to me, and then he had to leave so that he could drive Sahger to work.

Later, I heard Frank talking with his friends and he told them that when he first kissed me my mouth remained wide open until a fly almost died in it. Hearing that made me so upset I didn't want to see him, because he knew that I was still a child that had never been kissed, and for him to say that was shameful, horrible, and very upsetting, so I decided not to talk to him.

Frank started getting worried, because he did not know why I did not want to talk to him, so he asked Markadi to ask me what was wrong. After explaining to Markadi what happened, she told him, and he sent her to ask me to please meet with him downstairs in Pamala's house so we could talk. I told Markadi that I would be there when I was done my housework. After I finished, I went downstairs and there he was, looking so good, handsomely well-dressed, and after seeing him, I could not stay mad for long.

So he told me that he didn't say what he said to hurt me; he was only explaining how innocent I was and how he had to be very careful or else he would get into trouble with my mother. We settled things and I had to quickly run upstairs before my mother got home, because that could get me in really big trouble with her. While I was going about my normal day a few days after our conversation, Frank went ahead and bought me Levi's jeans and gave them to me as a gift.

With shaking hands, I took them and said thanks, but then I asked him what I should tell my mother when she asked who gave them to me. He said to tell her that it was a female friend. I took the jeans into the house and tried them on, but they were excessively big for me because they were for a young woman and I was not even a teenager yet.

My mother knew every piece of clothing she ever bought for me, so there was no way that the jeans could have been in our apartment without her noticing, so I was forced to show her. She asked me how and where I got them. I lied and said that Markadi gave them to me. My mother looked at the jeans for a long time and said to me, "I am going to send Chakakuka to call Markadi so I can ask her if what you say is true."

Chakakuka and Yahgahbo already knew it was Frank who gave me the jeans, but no one told on me because they all had their own secrets to hide from our mother, so my brother went along with the pretense and called Markadi, and on their way he told her why my mother had sent for her. When Markadi arrived, she knew exactly what answer to give to my mother.

When my mother asked Markadi if she was the one who gave me the jeans, she said yes, she did, and my mother told her that she would have to take them back because they were not my size, and besides, I had a lot of clothes to wear and I wouldn't be needing them. Markadi took the jeans and off she went. My mother was not satisfied about the jeans situation, so she warned me never to take anything from anyone. I told her OK and went about doing my housework.

Later my mother left the house for her outing. Chakakuka went to see Chichi and Yahgahbo went to see Chake and I was left home alone. Later, I heard a knock on the door, and when I asked who it was it turned out to be Frank. I happily opened the door and we sat outside on the stairs and talked. He told me that Markadi returned the jeans to him and he took them to the lady he bought them from and she refunded him his money.

He said he paid two hundred and fifty dollars for the jeans, and since my mother wouldn't allow me to have them, he brought me the money so I could use it to buy whatever I wanted. Being just a child, the money was too much for me and I was afraid that if my mother caught me with it she would kill me. Frank convinced me to take the money, so I did. When he left, I called Chakakuka and Yahgahbo and showed them the money. They were in shock.

I shared the money between us, and Chakakuka gave some of his money to Chichi. Yahgahbo, Chichi, Rere, and I went to the road to buy things we wanted, and when we returned home we had so much fun.

It seemed like the guys in the area were starting to check Chichi out, and Chakakuka didn't like that so they begin to have arguments. Yahgahbo's friend Rere had a crush on my sister's boyfriend Chake, so Yahgahbo and Rere stopped being friends.

Everyone was having their own issues. I wasn't focused on that because, although I liked Frank, I wasn't thinking about anything more than what we had: good communication. In addition, I was just too busy to be occupied with things that were not really any of my business. As we got used to the area, my mother began sending me to the markets all by myself, and I knew my way back and forth. All the women in the market liked me very much, because they thought that a little girl able to go to the market all by herself and know exactly what to buy was pretty amazing. All the women gave me the best when I went to buy things.

One day while Chakakuka and Yahgahbo were at school, I cleaned up the entire house and washed all the dishes. The only thing remaining was to cook the food, so I decided to go over to Jahjah's house for a bit to play with her kids before I headed to the market, since it was still too early. While playing at Jahjah's house with her kids, I realized that it had gotten late and I should have already gone to the market and been back and cooking already, so I freaked out and told Jahjah how much trouble I was in for being late. Jahjah told me not to worry, and that if my mother asked I should just tell her I was over at her house playing with her kids. I quickly got up and ran to the market, which was a distance away. It took me an hour to get to the market and it would take another hour to return.

While in the market, I was in such a rush to return home and start cooking, I forgot the house keys in the marketplace. When I returned home I realized that the keys were missing. Very worried, I ran back to the market, and because the ladies there loved me very much they had kept my keys for me, so when I arrived they give me my keys and I went running back home, but by the time I returned it was very late and Chakakuka and Yahgahbo had already been home awhile awaiting me.

It was a good thing that they had keys to enter the house, so when I got home I asked them to help me so that I did not get in trouble. They did help me to prepare the food, but it was not ready in time, so when my mother got home she knew that I had just started cooking. While she was asking me questions, like why I was cooking late, Pamala walked in and said, "Where is that one who called herself a little woman?"

My mother told her I was right there, and that she was wondering why I had just started cooking when I had all day to cook. Pamala started to make things worse for me; she told my mother how I had been gone all morning and all day, and how she had been looking for me but I was nowhere to be found.

She told my mother that she suspected that maybe I had been over to some guy's place, and that he had been fingering me. With no questions asked, my mother took the food that I was cooking and threw it over the balcony. Then she took a wooden fufu spoon and whipped me with it very badly, and as if that was not enough, she took her belt and beat me with it. She beat me so badly that I looked like a criminal punished for a crime I did not commit. It was sad that I was never given the chance to explain what happened and why the food was not ready on time.

Just at that time, Jahjah came over to my mother's apartment to check up on me, because she knew I was late to cook for my mother. She came to talk to her and to make her understand that I had spent the whole day over at her house playing with her kids. When Jahjah saw what my mother had done to me, she broke down and started crying and said she didn't know that my mother could be this wicked to a child. After learning that I had spent all day at Jahjah's place, my mother was very ashamed, but she still did not tell me she was sorry for what she did.

She just said, "Well, she should have told me that she was over at your place." Jahjah asked her, "But did you give her the chance to explain?" My mother did not answer, she just told me to get my ugly self from in front of her and go and take my bath. Jahjah was so mad for what my mother had done to me that she told my mother that she wouldn't be staying, that she had to leave because she couldn't stand the sight of me looking like that. Pamala, so ashamed for what she has done, said to me, "Well, next time, before you leave the house to go anywhere when your mother is not here, you come and tell me where it is you are going, that way I won't think you were out there doing something you got no business doing."

I was so mad at Pamala; I did not like her much after that day. There were marks all over my body and my eyes were swollen because my mother nearly destroyed my eye while she was beating me up. Frank learned what happened to me and he was not very happy about it, but he had to be very careful now when coming to see me, because he knew now for sure that if my mother caught him she would definitely kill him with her bare hands.

I kept away from people as much as possible, because I didn't want them seeing how badly I was beaten up, and the only time I ever went out was when I had to go to the market to buy food to cook for the house. When I left the house to buy food, the people who lived in the yard saw me and said, "We heard about the way your mother beat you up for nothing and we are so sorry she beat you like this," and that would have me feeling sorrier for myself. As time went by, I began to heal and all the marks on my skin started to go away.

Pamala was always coming over to ask for my mother; they became best friends, and they were always going out to places together. When Sahger came home, there was no Pamala—she was always out somewhere with my mother. What Pamala didn't know was that my mother was trying to get her in trouble with Sahger so that he would leave her, then my mother would have a chance to be his girlfriend.

Apparently, my mother had to tell the white man who worked with the American embassy about us being her daughters, and, as the story goes, he did not take it too well. We later found out that he was upset and told our mother that it would be hard for him to ever trust her again. He told her that he would pay her rent for one year, but she would need to find someone else after. I never got to meet him.

# CHAPTER 17

# THE PERFECT BETRAYAL; A BROKEN TRUST

My mother came home one day and went straight into her bedroom crying. I always knew when she was crying or not in a very good mood, because I paid attention to her. She told us that day that she did not want to be disturbed and that we should go out to play. Chakakuka and Yahgahbo were happy to have the privilege to go out and play, but I knew something was wrong. When she thought we had all gone out to play, she started to cry bitterly in her room and now I knew something was terribly wrong.

I knocked on her door to try to talk to her, but she told me she was not feeling too well and that she would talk to me later when she felt better. She didn't tell me anything later that day, instead she went over to Jahjah's place and explained to her what happened, and how stressed and worried she was because the man who was paying her rent and taking care of everything was no longer going to pay her rent and take care of us.

My mother also told Pamala about what happened, and they had their girls' talk. I am sure they found a solution to the problem, because the next day my mother seemed OK, but she wasn't in her usual happy mood. I kept my distance as much as possible so that I was not in her way to get beaten up or punished for something I did not do.

I kept the house clean and cooked food on time, and though I was home alone and Chakakuka and Yahgahbo were at school, I felt bad about the way my mother treated me differently. I think my mother needed some time to tell us what was going on, so after a week or so she called us to a meeting in the living room and told us that her American guy friend who'd been helping her out was no longer going to be there for us.

He had agreed that after the lease was over, he was going to pay for another year's rent but that would be it, because after that he was no longer going to be there. We felt sad, but, hey, I had never met this person so there was no emotional attachment to him as a father figure that I was going to miss; I only felt sad because I knew that would leave my mother feeling stressed. After the meeting, we went ahead with our daily activities as usual, because we knew at the end of the day my mother would take care of this.

After the beating my mother gave me, Frank was not coming around much anymore. When I tried to talk to him he kept himself really busy, and although I had feelings for him, I kept myself busy focusing on what was important, which was for me to do what was needed to be done and to stay out of trouble with my mother as much as possible.

One day while we were home, my mother brought home a male visitor we had never seen before, and his name was Mr. Hap. He was a very good-looking light-skinned man who had money and was well put together, but the problem was that he was married. I know you are probably wondering how I knew, and whether my mother told me, and my answer for you is no, my mother did not tell me anything, but his finger did.

On his left hand was a wedding ring, so it was very clear that he was indeed a married man, and I think my mother was the lover his wife knew nothing about. After introducing us, my mother sent us to our room and later came in and told us not to come outside or even disturb her about anything. Chakakuka, for some reason, thought that if the man liked our mother that would mean she would not be there to give him the attention he needed as the only male in the house, so he came up with a plan.

His plan was to poop in the toilet, and when Mr. Hap asked to use the washroom there would be poop waiting for him to see, and he would get really upset and never come back. I wasn't sure how that plan was going to work, but I didn't want to be part of it thinking about how much of a beating I always received from her, so Chakakuka carried out his plan on his own. He pooped in the toilet and didn't flush it, so when it came time for Mr. Hap to use the washroom, my mother called him, saying, "Chakakuka, go and make sure the washroom is clean, because Mr. Hap would like to use it."

Chakakuka said OK, and then came back to my mother and told her that the washroom was all clean and ready to be used, and my mother said OK and sent him back into the room. When he came back in, he told us that he put a very big load of shit down and it was just a matter of time until we would hear Mr. Hap scream. Sure enough, it wasn't long before we heard a big scream out of the washroom.

Mr. Hap couldn't believe what his eyes were seeing and screamed for my mother to come and see it. When my mother went into to the washroom, Mr. Hap said this was broad-daylight witchcraft, and whoever did this was extremely wicked and that he was going to leave and never come back. My mother tried to beg Mr. Hap to stay, but he refused and insisted that he wanted to leave.

However, before he left my mother called us outside and, with tears in her eyes, asked which one of us did such a horrible act, and we told her it was her son Chakakuka. She made him apologize to Mr. Hap, but his apology was not enough to make Mr. Hap stay or to ever come back. I just knew that after Mr. Hap left Chakakuka was going to get the beating of his life, and yep, he did.

She beat him so badly. She wanted to kill him for being that wicked, but, hey, it was her own favourite child who messed up her love life, and thank God I didn't agree to join him because who knows the level of beating I would have received. I think at that point she'd had more than enough from her only son and could not stand it anymore. She decided that he was not allowed outside the bedroom for a week. The only thing Chakakuka was allowed to do was eat his food in the room, sleep, and use the very same washroom he used to drive Mr. Hap away.

For me, it was fun seeing him finally being punished by his beloved mother, because most of the time she allowed him to get away with a lot of stuff, but this time it was her turn to enjoy a piece of the rotten pie she had been keeping protected, and it did not taste good. It was to my taste to see him locked up in the room for a week, because that meant more freedom for me, and if he dared to go outside the room for anything other than to use the washroom we were ordered to make a report when she returned.

You should have seen him bored out of his head; he did not know what to do with his time locked up in the room. When my mother got home after three days of him being in the room, he tried to beg her for a lesser punishment, but she said her punishment stays and that he should return to the room. Jahjah and Pamala came to visit my mother, and when she explained what happened to them, they were very mad at Chakakuka.

They just couldn't believe what he did, and they laughed very hard when my mother told them how loud the man screamed just because he saw my brother's poop in the toilet. Chakakuka was standing there because they called him out of the room to ask him why he did such wickedness to his mother. When my mother was explaining about Mr. Hap screaming at the top of his lungs, Chakakuka wanted to laugh, and my mother told him that just because her friends were laughing it didn't make it funny.

"If you dare laugh here, I will break your head to pieces." My mother sent me for her belt in the room, and though her friends begged her and told her his punishment was enough, she said, "No, I don't think it was," and she give him a good whipping again. After she was done, her friends told him how his behaviour was very wrong and that he should truly apologize to his mother. My mother's friends stayed over for a while and then left for their own homes.

After Chakakuka completed his punishment in the room, he was asked to come outside and apologize to his mother. I'm not sure if our friends got all the details, but the only thing they knew for sure was that my mother had beaten him up and that he was in the room for a week. When he was out, he started explaining to our friends what happened and they all laughed, saying how Chakakuka was a badass to scare the guy away. They gave him high-fives and that had me so mad.

I knew that if my mother had the same opportunity as other women she wouldn't have dated a married man, but she needed help taking care of us so that was why she was trying to encourage a married man and bring him home. So I told Chakakuka that if he thought what he did was funny, he should just keep talking about it and I would be the one to tell Mama that he was not sorry for what he did.

"I will tell her that you were proudly telling your friends about what you did and you were all laughing about it and they were giving you high-fives." Chakakuka stopped talking about it and we went about our normal day-to-day life, hanging out and playing with friends. My mother and Pamala were hanging out every day, and Pamala forgot that she had a man to take care of. Most times when Pamala went out with my mother, their maid would be the one to cook for Sahger.

When Sahger would get home and ask about the whereabouts of Pamala, the maid would tell him that Pamala had been out all day with my mother and hadn't come home yet. Pamala would sometimes come home very late in the morning, and even though we lived upstairs, we could still hear them argue with each other. During the day, they would walk past one another as if they did not know each other. Sahger warned Pamala to lessen how much time she spent with my mother and told her that he did not want her coming home very late.

Pamala paid no attention to Sahger's warning, got carried away by my mother's entertaining personality, and kept going out to parties with her. My mother had her own master plan that Pamala knew nothing about. From the looks of things, I think my mother had a crush on Sahger, but I did not think she would ever do Pamala wrong because of how close they were as friends.

I guess that because she was a single mother in Africa with three kids to take care of and no job, all she ever thought about was how to survive. It didn't matter if she were to lose someone's trust or break someone's heart. Something started to go wrong with their friendship. I think it all happened while they were out partying and was over who was getting more attention.

Pamala started spending less time with my mother and more time at home, but one day all hell broke loose. I'm not sure what the reason was, but one morning they started to have what you would call a little argument which then turned into a huge argument. While in the process of that, they started to relive everything they used to do together and Sahger learned how Pamala cheated on him with other men while hanging out with my mother.

For Sahger that was a no, being a Muslim man, and he could no longer keep Pamala as his woman. He had to let her go, because the news had already spread faster than a wildfire, and she did not just break his heart but she brought him huge disgrace as a man who supported her financially and much more. After a few days of arguing and other people trying to tell Pamala and Sahger to fix their relationship, Pamala moved some of her things over to her father's house and spent the time over there until she could figure things out.

I got extremely sad over what was going on, because I did like Pamala very much, and to see her go like that pained me a lot. The day that Pamala packed some of her things and left, Sahger was very upset so he also left and probably did not come home until it was very late that night. I remember that the next morning Sahger was home alone, because I didn't see the maid come in, or anyone, for that matter. The next thing I knew, my mother said that she was going to go down to Sahger's place to try to talk to him about making things work with Pamala.

So, she went downstairs, and I think their conversation was going really well because my mother sent one of her errand boys upstairs to tell me that if we needed anything she would be downstairs sitting in Sahger's place.

Sahger was expecting visitors so my mother came upstairs, but she was looking very pleased so I thought she had settled things with Sahger and Pamala, and that Pamala would be coming home soon, but that was the opposite of what happened. Well, my mother had a very good day at home, and then later went to visit with some friends, and when she came home later that evening Sahger sent his driver Frank to tell my mother that he wanted to see her.

My mother got herself ready and downstairs she went to Sahger's place. I thought my mother was coming home later so I waited up for her, but she didn't come home, so I knew she would be sleeping over at Sahger's place. I was upset that she could betray her own close friend Pamala like that. I fell asleep later on, but I made sure to wake up early because I wanted to confirm where it was my mother had slept, and I was not much surprised when I saw her creeping out of Sahger's place with his white T-shirt on and nothing underneath it.

As soon as she came up the stairs, I ran to our bedroom and pretended to be fast asleep on the bed beside Chakakuka and Yahgahbo. When she came inside the apartment, she did not try waking us up because she thought all of us were still asleep and she did not want us figuring out that she did not sleep at home. She went into her bedroom, changed clothes, and then woke us up, saying, "I just cannot believe that you all still sleeping at this time of the day when there is a lot of work to do around the house."

She had Chakakuka and Yahgahbo clean and wash dishes while she sent me into the market to buy food so she could cook. When I returned from the market, my mother cooked and took food to Sahger, and said that since Pamala was not around, she would help cook him food.

I just knew something was up between the two of them, but I could not put my finger on it. I knew deeply that they were doing Pamala wrong and it really upset me, but, hey, what can I say, I was just a little girl who was learning to understand people and why they reacted in such ways. I told Chakakuka and Yahgahbo about what I observed, and as they took a closer look at the situation they started to see that I was right, and they were also not in support of her doing that to Pamala.

We dared not say a word about it, so most times we saw and heard things as if we did not. Pamala returned for a few days to pack the rest of her stuff so she could leave Sahger for good, and when my mother saw her, she did not even greet her. They both walked past one another as if they weren't friends before. My mother stood upstairs on the balcony to watch as Pamala removed her stuff from Sahger's apartment.

When Pamala noticed my mother watching her from upstairs, she said something and my mother replied, and the next thing we knew they were swearing at one another. As the swearing continued, my mother went into her kitchen and poured water on Pamala from up above. Pamala was very upset so she came upstairs for a fight, but my mother refused to open the door for her. She promised my mother that she would wait until she went downstairs and then they would get into a fight.

My mother accepted the challenge and came down for the fight, and it was a much-said thing to watch two people who once cared about each other but were now bitter enemies. I know news spreads faster than a wildfire, and somewhere, somehow, Pamala heard that Sahger and my mother had something going on, so she started to insult my mother, even calling her cheap and very low. Nevertheless, my mother responded by saying that Pamala was the low one—living with a man and having affairs out of her home. With all the tension that was going on, I still saw Pamala as a person I cared deeply for. When Pamala left, I cried because I knew I would not be seeing her and her sister Markadi again, or at least not anytime soon. I was upset at my mother because I knew the breakup of Pamala and Sahger was her fault.

Well, for me things were not going to be the same, because Pamala cared about me, too, and she would always give me stuff or buy stuff for me, and to me she was a big sister and a friend. My mother and Sahger were now very close, and she was always at Sahger's place. Even when he had visitors, they would be there laughing, talking, drinking, and having a good time. My mother barely spent any time at home with us; we were taking care of ourselves, and for the time she did spend at home with us, she was either yelling at us or we were being punished for stuff she said we did wrong.

Apparently, Sahger promised my mother that he would be there for us and make sure that we were being taken care of by helping her financially. I was deeply sad by what was going on, and I just wanted something to change. Luckily for me, school was about to start, and this time around I was registered to attend along with Chakakuka and Yahgahbo. My mother got us registered in Cathedral Catholic School.

She got us all of our school supplies and school uniforms, including book bags for school. But before attending school, my mother gave me a very strong warning that if this time around I get kicked out of school for refusing to salute the flag, she would never register me in another school again, because she could not afford to waste her money foolishly.

I heard what my mother said and was very careful not to be kicked out of school this time around. With all the new stuff I got for school, I was so excited to start and to get to meet and make new friends, but most especially to learn, because I did not get to go to school for two years. I was behind a bit, but I always read more and studied when I was at home alone, making sure to prepare myself for when school started.

School started, and the first day was all about in-class introductions, but being a friendly person, I had already made a few friends by the time the day ended. At school, we did what you would call devotion every morning, where we all stood out in the schoolyard in a lineup and the entire school saluted the national flag, said the national anthem, and then said prayers and heard announcements about school activities. The devotion was every morning before classes started.

While standing in line for devotion, most of the students liked to stand with their friends from the same class. Sometimes some of the students would even leave their devotion line to stand with their friends from another class, and when that happened, students would talk, laugh, and not pay any attention to what was going on, so teachers started looking for such students and separating them from one another. In class, it was so much fun getting to know the other students and the teachers.

There were girls who acted as if they were sitting on top of the world, but it did not trouble me at all, because I became friends with girls who became friends with me. We had twelve teachers for twelve subjects, but our favourite teacher was Mr. Hard. If I am not mistaken, he was our geography teacher. Mr. Hard always came to class drunk, but he was a good drunk, because other teachers could not tell, only his students knew. We all had so much fun and he made geography a fun subject to study. There were other teachers who were quite nice, and others were mean and aggressive to students.

Apart from Mr. Hard, we had other favourite teachers, too, but I have forgotten their names. At home, life was normal, and as usual my mother was always gone, but being in school kept us very busy studying and playing less. On the weekends, we got to play with our friends more because my mother warned us not to fail. At home, I made sure to do all my housework, including going to the market to buy food to cook before studying, because I did not want my mother coming home and seeing that nothing had been done, because then I would get into big trouble.

At school, the teacher had the right to discipline us if our uniform was dirty, our hair was not neatly fixed, or our homework was not completed. So, I made sure to always have my uniform clean, hair neatly fixed, and schoolwork completed. However, sometimes it was a challenge for me, because of the household duties I had to complete before doing anything for myself. Sometimes I did go to school with incomplete schoolwork.

Moreover, if the teacher requested all homework in and found ours incomplete, he would call us to stand in front of the class and give us a whipping on our butts or our hands, and when we cried the entire class laughed at us.

I got embarrassed like that in front of the entire class a few times, and it was not a good feeling. There were boys in my class that liked me, but I did not pay any attention to them, I saw them as more like brothers or friends because they were always doing, or trying to do, something stupid to the girls. For example, there was this school pencil sharpener that was round with a mirror on it, and the boys in the class would roll the sharpener under the girls' chairs and they would tell you that they had come to pick up their sharpener. Then they would look in the mirror to see what colour panties the girls were wearing. After they found out, they would tell their friends and they would all laugh. When we found out what was going on, we told our teachers. It wasn't just in our class this was happening, other classes were experiencing the same thing, so the school principal banned the pencil sharpener from being sold at the school and from anyone being in possession of it.

He promised to expel anyone owning the sharpener from the school. I never did pay any attention to the boys at school, but there was one particular boy I had a crush on. He was half Lebanese, half Liberian, and his name was Shahem. Every morning when I got to school, I would make sure to walk past his classroom a few times during class, and then on my lunch break, just so he would notice me, but he paid no attention to me because he had no knowledge that I had feelings for him.

To my surprise, Pamala's sister Markadi started attending my school; she and Shahem were in the same class, and she chatted with most of the boys in her class, including Shahem. I now had a master plan to getting Shahem's attention.

My plan was to get Markadi to tell Shahem that I liked him and that I would like to have a word with him. At home, I just could not wait to get to school and have a talk with Markadi. The morning came and I went to school in search of Markadi, but when I got into her class, I noticed Shahem was not sitting far from Markadi, and that was perfect. I told Markadi what I had planned, and she agreed to carry out my plan for me, and that had me all excited but I did not know how it was going to be carried out.

It was during lunchtime, and just as I had left my classroom to go for lunch, I saw Markadi and Shahem talking in front of their classroom. As I walked past them, Markadi called me, and in front of Shahem, said, "Here he is, you said you had something to tell him, right?" I did not know what to say to Shahem; I did not know what to say to a boy at all, because I had no experience.

I just stood there, speechless; I did not know what to say to a boy I had been deeply liking for a while. So, as I collected of myself, I remember telling him, "Who me? No, I did not tell her that," then I ran away. Later that day, during school hours, I met up with Markadi and she said to me, "If you knew you did not want to talk to Shahem, then why did you ask me to speak to him on your behalf?" I said that I did want to talk to him, but I was too shy and did not know what to say to him.

Ever since that day, every time I saw Shahem in school, I ran or took a different direction because I felt embarrassed at him knowing that I had feelings for him. At home, life seemed settled and things were taken care of. I must say, despite my mother being a single mother of three, I wasn't one hundred percent sure how she did it, but she did it. She took very good care of us and we attended good schools.

My mother was not around most of the time, and I had to become the next mother in the house at a very young age. I was very proud of her in some ways, and in some ways I was not proud of some of the things she did. Living with my mother, I lost my childhood. I did not know how to be a kid or act as a kid, because I was too busy being the mother to Chakakuka and Yahgahbo.

They were always off playing most times, and the only times they were ever around to help me was when I complained about them not helping me. My mother, for all her ways, was a loving mother in the way she knew how to be. She did not have a perfect childhood, so being a single mother to three children was a challenge and a struggle for her, and she probably did not know how to love us right, like the way any mother from a well-structured home should love her kids.

However, she showed her love in many different ways. Most times she struggled with mood swings, where one minute she was happy and the next minute she was sad. Nevertheless, I understood her more than anyone who ever came close to her. She felt abandoned and helpless, and though she loved us, she found it hard to show it because she had been so busy worrying about how we would all survive. When she was in her good moods we all had fun at home, and sometimes she even took us out to get ice cream or to the beach.

Sometimes, we all did the cooking and cleaning together, and while doing the cleaning we would play music and she would take the broom and pretend that it was a microphone. Nevertheless, when she got in a bad mood, we stayed on our best behaviour and made sure not to cause any trouble, because she would just take all of her frustration out on us. My mother was a very beautiful, attractive woman who made the room stop when she walked into a gathering or an occasion, and her attractiveness kept her from having too many friends.

Her attractiveness intimidated most of her friends, because she got all the attention wherever they went. My mother had a temper that most people did not understand. She experienced a very rough life, and because of that, she was always so very protective of herself and her kids. With her walls being up so high, it was hard for anyone to get close to her, and even the ones who were close to her walked on eggshells for fear that at any wrong click she would explode.

We as children got most of her frustration, because we were the ones around when she released it, but I for one always forgave her no matter what. Some of her judgement about the way she made her sacrifices to be there for us was not right, but, hey, she was a whole lot better than those mothers who abandoned their kids or were never there for them. For all she ever did for us, I have been truly grateful for everything she has ever been through because of us. Sitting here writing this just put a smile on my face as I thought about it.

Sometimes it was even hard to show her how much we loved her, because we weren't sure when she was going to flip or if what we did might upset her, but we still loved her and always will. As we grew up and I learned things so fast, my mother did not like how transparent she was to me, and how I saw all of her imperfections. What she did not know was that, no matter how transparent she was to me or how imperfect she was, I still truly love her for how brave and caring she had been to us.

We never get to choose the parents we were born to, but we get to understand them, love them, care for them, and forgive them for all of the things that they did not do right for us, and do it right for ourselves so that we do not have ourselves to blame later on, as well.

Months went by and our school got a new principal. His name was Mr. Alexander. Mr. Alexander was a former principal at the St. Edward

School, and seeing him now at Cathedral School was a surprise, but it felt good to have a former principal at our current school. Mr. Alexander realized after being at the school for a couple of months that the students were out of hand, basically doing whatever they wanted to a certain level. Students were coming to school with dirty uniforms, hair not fixed neatly, dirty socks, and worn-out shoes.

Boys who were developing facial hair were also not shaving properly, and students were coming to school really late and there were teachers taking barbs from students to give them passing grades. Mr. Alexander decided that there had to be straight rules that everyone needed to follow. Now, we all know it is not always easy getting everyone to do what is right, and soon Mr. Alexander created many enemies for himself at school, both with teachers and with students.

Mr. Alexander started to change most of the rules at the school, leaving the students with less freedom. If you were a girl student and your hair wasn't combed or braided properly, it didn't matter how early you got to school, you would be asked to either stand outside the fence gate and braid it neatly, or you could go home and come back the next day. It was the same with the boys who started to develop facial hair; they were asked to shave, or they could remain at home.

As time went by, Mr. Alexander had the school shaping up the way he wanted it to be. Some students followed the rules, but as we all know, not all students were going to respect them. Some who disrespected the rules got punished, there was no joke about that. I made a few friends in school and in my class, but I am unable to remember their names, because it has been so long. I started to get popular in school, and soon all the teachers and students knew who I was because of my active personality.

There were boys in senior classes who used to check me out, and when the teachers were having meetings, they would send the senior students over to the elementary and junior high side of the school to substitute for the teachers while they were away. The boys in the senior class always substituted junior classes of girls they had crushes on. Most times when they would come to class, they tried to show that they were in charge. Sometimes, even if the teacher gave them a different class to monitor, they would switch classes with their other senior classmates just so they could be in the same class with the girl they had a crush on.

My mother was busy with her own life and I was busy at school, but that did not mean I was not allowed to do any housework. I still did my household duties after school each day so that I did not get in trouble with my mother for not having the house clean and for not cooking anything for her to eat.

Most evenings when I did my housework early, I would sit on the top of the back balcony and study, then complete my school assignments for the next day. Chakakuka made many friends at school and most of them were mixed, just the same as him, and they were very good looking, but my brother had rules that none of his friends were allowed to mess with his sisters. In addition, if he ever noticed anything like that, the friendship between him and the friend was over, so because of that his friends kept away from us.

Their communication with us was "hello" and "goodbye." I did not have the chance to establish any facial contact with any of his friends, because none of them were willing to lose their friendship with Chakakuka for my sake. My mother made a new friend name Fossia, and she had a sister name Biata, and they had little brothers, too, but I cannot remember their names.

I am pretty sure my mother and Fossia became friends because my mother started dating Fossia's stepdad and Fossia was unaware of it. Fossia's mother was in the USA, and because Fossia was old enough to care for her brothers and sister, she was in charge, but my mother was the one who oversaw a lot of things for them because she was introduced as a family friend and a business partner.

Fossia and my mother became close friends and we were allowed to go there for visits. My mother told us to make sure to let her know when we would like to go over for visit and to make sure to return home on time for bed. We were not allowed to come home very late, because my mother said the roads were very dangerous at night and unsafe for kids to walk alone, but most times when we went over for visit, we ended up coming home late at night.

The lucky thing for us was that, on all the nights we came home late, my mother was not home so we did not get in trouble. Fossia and Biata's parents' house was huge, and because their parents were in the USA at the time, they always sent stuff for them to Liberia, so Biata and her siblings had fancy things from the USA, including toys for the boys. Because of that, every day when we were finished school, we made sure the house was clean and the food was cooked, then off to Biata and Fossia's house we went. But one day, luck was not on our side.

We were busy playing until we forgot the time and it had gotten very late. With that in mind, and the punishment we were going to face, we begged Fossia to come with us to tell our mother that we spent all day at their house, but Fossia said that she would come to the house the next day. She said that we should not worry much, and that my mother would not beat us just because we visited them.

Before we could leave their compound to go home, my mother was already downstairs with her belt to beat us. Fossia came downstairs to talk to my mother and to let her know it was a simple mistake, but my mother refused to listen, whipping us a bit instead and threatening to whip us some more when we got home. When we got home, we were beaten and banned from going over to play, because my mother said we were not responsible enough to leave the house and return home on time.

Sometimes we only went over to visit when Biata came to ask my mother to go over, or if my mother was visiting she would take us. Fossia and Biata started getting ready for their trip to the USA along with their brothers, but something happened. I'm not sure what went wrong, but Fossia found out that my mother was her stepdad's mistress and she decided that she no longer wanted to be close friends with her.

She even stopped her brothers and her sister Biata from coming to visit us. Well, that was the end to another friendship. Our lease at the apartment was almost over and the property owner said that after the lease ended there would be an increase in rent if my mother wanted to continue renting. My mother got in contact with an aunty of hers who owned an apartment complex in Monrovia, Liberia, but who lived in the USA. She was unable to manage it from such a distance and needed someone who was going to make sure that things were well at the apartments.

She also needed someone who would collect the rent from the renters, so she assigned my mother as her trusted person to do just that. While still at the apartment, a guest came from America and my mother knew him.

His name was Mr. Bamilton; he was familiar with our family and he had come to Liberia to settle his family problem and would not be staying very long. I'm not sure how she got the news, but she said that a family friend from America was visiting, that she was going over to greet him, and if anyone asked for her I should go over to call her. My mother started spending a lot of time over at the place where Mr. Bamilton was staying for his visit to Liberia, even not coming home at night most times, claiming she was helping at the house along with the other family members.

I believed that she was only helping because when people come from America or other European countries they usually need extra help. One day while at home going about my normal housework, there was a knock on our door, and when I opened it there stood my grandmother Stuciah. What a surprise that was. She never paid us visits, so seeing her standing in front of the door with a big smile on her face asking me how I was doing surprised me.

I was at a loss for words and did not know what to tell her, so I welcomed her in happily and offered her food and a drink. She asked where my mother was, and I told her that she was not home. That is when she told me that she heard Mr. Bamilton was in Liberia and that my mother knew where he was staying, so she came so that my mother could take her there. I knew the name sounded familiar but could not place a proper story to it.

While I was wondering who this Mr. Bamilton was and how he was related to my family, my grandmother Stuciah started to explain the story. She had told me many years ago when I was very little about a man she was madly in love with, but I could not remember how their relationship ended. There was a special song they had for one another and that was their love song.

The song goes like this: "John Clakey Vla-ka-vlu-ku," and the minute she started singing I remembered the story all too well, and how much my grandmother Stuciah have loved this man. I had tears in my eyes, knowing that the man my grandmother Stuciah had loved all these years was now here and that the two of them could finally meet once again. I told my grandmother Stuciah that I knew where he was staying and that the place was just across from where we lived.

My grandmother Stuciah was very excited and could not wait to see the love of her life again, and I could not wait to see the both of them unite again. We hurriedly went over to where Mr. Bamilton was staying, and when we got there, he had many family members awaiting him in the living room. As we sat down to wait, some of Mr. Bamilton's family members who knew of my grandmother Stuciah's relationship with Mr. Bamilton started to whisper to one another.

My grandmother Stuciah and I were not sure what their whispers were about, but my grandmother Stuciah just thought they were whispering because they thought she was there to beg Mr. Bamilton for money. My grandmother Stuciah said to me, "I did not come here to beg him for money, but they are not the only ones who need his money after all these years of being gone; I, too, deserve it, because he was my man." We sat a bit but there were still whispers going on in the living room.

My grandmother Stuciah told me to go and call my mother to let her know that she was out in the living room. I asked one of the family members for the whereabouts of my mother, and they told me that she was busy having a meeting with Mr. Bamilton and that they would let her know that I had requested her. When I returned, my grandmother Stuciah asked if I had the chance to give my mother her message. I said no, that she was in a meeting with Mr. Bamilton.

After a few minutes, my mother sent one of Mr. Bamilton's family members to call me into the room. When I got into the room, my mother asked me why I was there and I told her that her mother Stuciah came looking for her and asked that I bring her over. My mother said, "What! You mean to tell me you brought her over here?" I said, "But you did not tell me not to bring anyone over here and she came to meet Mr. Bamilton, because she heard that he had come from America."

With all this being said, I could not help but notice that my mother was in Mr. Bamilton's bedroom wearing just a white T-shirt and her panties. My mother told me to go back outside and tell my grandmother Stuciah that she would be right out, so I left to give my grandmother her message. Mr. Bamilton was not at home at the time, which is why everyone was awaiting him.

While my mother was still in the bedroom, Mr. Bamilton arrived, and for a second I thought he was going to happily greet my grandmother Stuciah, but he briefly greeted her and told her that he would be right back so they could talk, and off to his bedroom he went. Not long after Mr. Bamilton went into his bedroom, my mother came outside, and to my surprise, she did not put any extra clothes on. She came walking out in front of everyone still wearing the white T-shirt and just her panties.

I was in a lot of shock, because knowing that my grandmother Stuciah was awaiting my mother out in the living room, and that there were other members of Mr. Bamilton's family sitting in the living room, should at least have given my mother the decency to put on proper clothing before coming out. At the sight of my mother coming out of Mr. Bamilton's bedroom with just a T-shirt and panties on, my grandmother knew then and there that my mother had had sex with Mr. Bamilton.

As I looked into my grandmother's eyes, I saw that they were blood red, with tears in them. With no remorse, my mother greeted her mother with a very rude attitude. My mother called her mother by the name Stuciah, a name most people knew my grandmother by. My mother said to her mother, "Stuciah, what is it you came to do here?" With great anger, my grandmother answered her, saying, "Well, I am here to see Bamilton, and why are you asking me that like I am not invited here?"

My grandmother was trying her hardest to keep her cool, but I could see that she was fighting back the tears and the pain. My mother then replied, saying, "Well, as you can see, he is busy, but I will talk to him so that he can see you." My grandmother Stuciah said, "I can see you are keeping him busy." Then all hell broke loose and they were at each other, yelling back and forth.

I ran outside to cry, because such a thing is painful to watch. While outside, I could still hear so much going on inside the house—people yelling and screaming at each other. After it was settled, my mother stayed in Mr. Bamilton's room and my grandmother was out in the living room having a talk with Mr. Bamilton. I'm not sure what they talked about, but he gave her some money and told her to come back to see him on a later date.

My grandmother Stuciah asked me to walk her to where she could take a taxi home, and as we walked she cried. When I asked her what was happening, she told me that I would not understand what was going on. What adults do not realize is that kids are smart, even smarter than adults, and though adults keep many secrets from kids most times, kids already know some of the things adults try to hide.

After making sure that my grandmother Stuciah got a taxi to take her home safely, I started to walk back home myself, and right before I could get to our house, my mother had sent someone to call me back to Mr. Bamilton's place. I got there, and when I asked for my mother, the people in the house told me that she was in the kitchen. I went to the kitchen, and my mother took me into the bedroom, and was very upset with me for bringing my grandmother over to the house.

I replied by telling her that I did tell my grandmother that my mother was busy, but she insisted that she wanted to meet with Mr. Bamilton. My mother said to me, "You should have told her that you did not know where Mr. Bamilton lives. Now your grandmother Stuciah came here and caused a scene by jumping me for a fight, and she got everyone talking." I just stood there not sure what to say. She told me, "Well, get home to your brother and sister; make sure they are OK and tell them that I will be home soon."

So, on my way home, I kept thinking about what was going on, why my grandmother Stuciah would jump my mother for a fight and why it looked like my mother was having a sexual relationship with a person who was an ex-boyfriend of my grandmother Stuciah's. It was not long before Mr. Bamilton had to return to America, so he asked to meet with us before leaving Liberia.

Chakakuka and Yahgahbo were unaware of what happened between my mother and my grandmother; all they ever knew was that Mr. Bamilton was a long-time ex-boyfriend of our grandmother Stuciah's and that he was visiting Liberia and would be returning to America shortly.

So we got to the house, and upon seeing Mr. Bamilton, Chakakuka and Yahgahbo could not help themselves. They were overwhelmed with excitement, knowing that Mr. Bamilton was and always had been the love of our grandmother Stuciah's life, and to see him in person was so amazing for them. I just sat there wondering about what happened earlier between my grandmother and my mother. Mr. Bamilton brought some stuff from America and handed some of it over to us; I cannot remember exactly what he gave us, but it was something nice.

He also gave us money, but my mother took it and said that she would keep it for us, that it was not good to give kids money. They gave us food to eat and some juice to drink, but we did not stay longer because there was more family coming over to visit Mr. Bamilton before he left for America, so my mother told us to go home. We said goodbye and home we went, but once we were home there were talks about how tall and good looking Mr. Bamilton was, and how now we could see what made our grandmother Stuciah love him so much.

While my brother and sister were busy talking and imagining our grandmother Stuciah and Mr. Bamilton getting back together, all I did was sit and wonder why my mother would do such a thing to her mother. Mr. Bamilton's visit to Liberia was finally over, but he promised my mother that he would be back, and that when he got his business plan together he would like to come back to Liberia to establish it and he would make sure to keep in contact with her while he was gone until he returned.

Nevertheless, that was the last my mother ever heard from Mr. Bamilton. After that day, we did not hear anything about him, and that was my first and last time ever seeing him.

# About the Author

Arnelle M. Cruz was born in Monrovia, Liberia, West Africa, and has been a writer ever since she was a child. Her mother never took any interest in her writing, but later Arnelle knew that she would write her own story.

She always knew that one day she would become very successful, and her experience with the war and trauma did not stop her dream.

Six months after she came to Canada, she made it on Canadian national TV and in national newspapers for Canadian Idol Season 2.

Her dream was short-lived because a *Canadian Idol* judge told her that her voice sounded worse than dogs barking in the street.

Though she didn't have the voice and accent the judges were looking for, she knew her voice was in her writing.

Her mother died in 2006, and two days before her mother died, Arnelle told her that she needed a pen and paper because there was something she needed to write.

She did not know what it was she wanted to write on the last night she got to spend with her mother, but six years after her mother's death, in 2012, she realized what she wanted to write.

What she wanted to write was the story of her life.

Manufactured by Amazon.ca
Bolton, ON

33919023R00125